Ripley's Believe It or Not!®

RIPLEY PUBLISHING

Ryan DeSear Vice President, Attraction Operations and Technology

Suzanne Smagala-Potts Senior Manager, Marketing and Communications

Editor Jordie R. Orlando

Project Manager Yaneisy Contreras

Junior Editor Maire Clayton

Snippet Text Geoff Tibballs

Feature Contributors Amanda Askew, Maire Clayton, Allyson Iovino, Jordan Neese, Jordie R. Orlando

Copy Editors Amanda Askew, Jordie R. Orlando

Fact-checkers Amanda Askew, Rachel Paul

Proofreader Rachel Paul

Indexer Amanda Askew

Designers Rose Audette, Ekechi Pitt

Reprographics Bob Prohaska

Cover Designers Julia Moellmann, Rose Audette

Special Thanks Leigh Adams, Gabby Barela, Tacita Barrera, Steve Campbell, Kieran Castaño, Kelsey Connolly, John Corcoran, Juan Fernandez, Jeff Goldman, Caleb Hagood, Colton Kruse, Matt Mamula, Bobby Orlando, Anthony Perry, Nicole Rodriguez, Bea Sejas

ISBN 978-1-60991-539-1

FSC
www.fsc.org
MIX
Paper | Supporting responsible forestry
FSC® C020056

For more information regarding permission, contact:
Ripley Entertainment Inc.
9545 S. John Young Parkway, Suite 222
Orlando, Florida 32819
publishing@ripleys.com
www.ripleys.com

Manufactured in China in May 2026 by Leo Paper

First Printing

Library of Congress Control Number: 2026935776

PUBLISHER'S NOTE
While every effort has been made to verify the accuracy of the entries in this book, the Publisher cannot be held responsible for any errors contained in the work. They would be glad to receive any information from readers.

WARNING
Some of the stunts and activities are undertaken by experts and should not be attempted by anyone without adequate training and supervision.

Ripley's Believe It or Not!®

WIRED INTO WEIRD

Ripley® Publishing
a Jim Pattison Company

WHAT'S

CONTENTS

Discover some of the rare and unusual items found in Ripley's Believe It or Not! Attractions around the globe.

Get to know the people behind the pictures in interviews you won't find anywhere else!

INSIDE?

FACT FILES

Find out even more about a story with these bonus bits of info!

EVERY DAY A HOLIDAY! ↗

Check the text at the bottom of pages to see what you could be celebrating each day!

↗ FAN SHARE

See what readers like you have shared with Ripley's!

YOU CAN BE IN A RIPLEY'S BOOK!

Do you have an unbelievable story, a unique talent, a one-of-a-kind pet, or a remarkable discovery? Share it with Ripley's for a chance to be featured!

Ripleys.com/Share

WIRED IN

Despite being around for more than 100 years, Ripley's Believe It or Not! stays on the cutting edge of technology. Here are just a few fun ways we've kept ourselves *Wired Into Weird*.

DANCING ROBOTS!

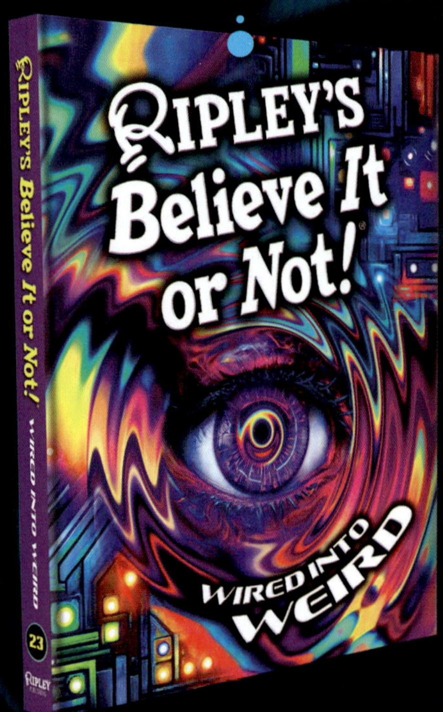

Blending Art and Tech

This book cover was put together by real human designers who used AI as a tool to help bring their artistic ideas to life. The artificial assistance was just one small part of process; a team of real people spent many hours refining, testing, and perfecting the design! And of course, all of the stories and photos inside the book are completely real. Believe It or Not!

Robot Takeover

Friendly robot dogs and dancing humanoids steal the spotlight and amaze guests at Ripley's Attractions around the world. The robot pup became such a fan favorite that a special contest was held to give it the perfect name: Glitch!

MEET GLITCH!

TO WEIRD

FUN INTERACTIVE TECH!

VIRTUAL WORLDS!

VERSE IMMERSIVE

Virtual Fun

Step into a new world with Verse Immersive at Ripley's Super Fun Park in Pigeon Forge, Tennessee! This high-tech adventure lets you solve puzzles, crack codes, and unlock mysteries in a fully interactive space.

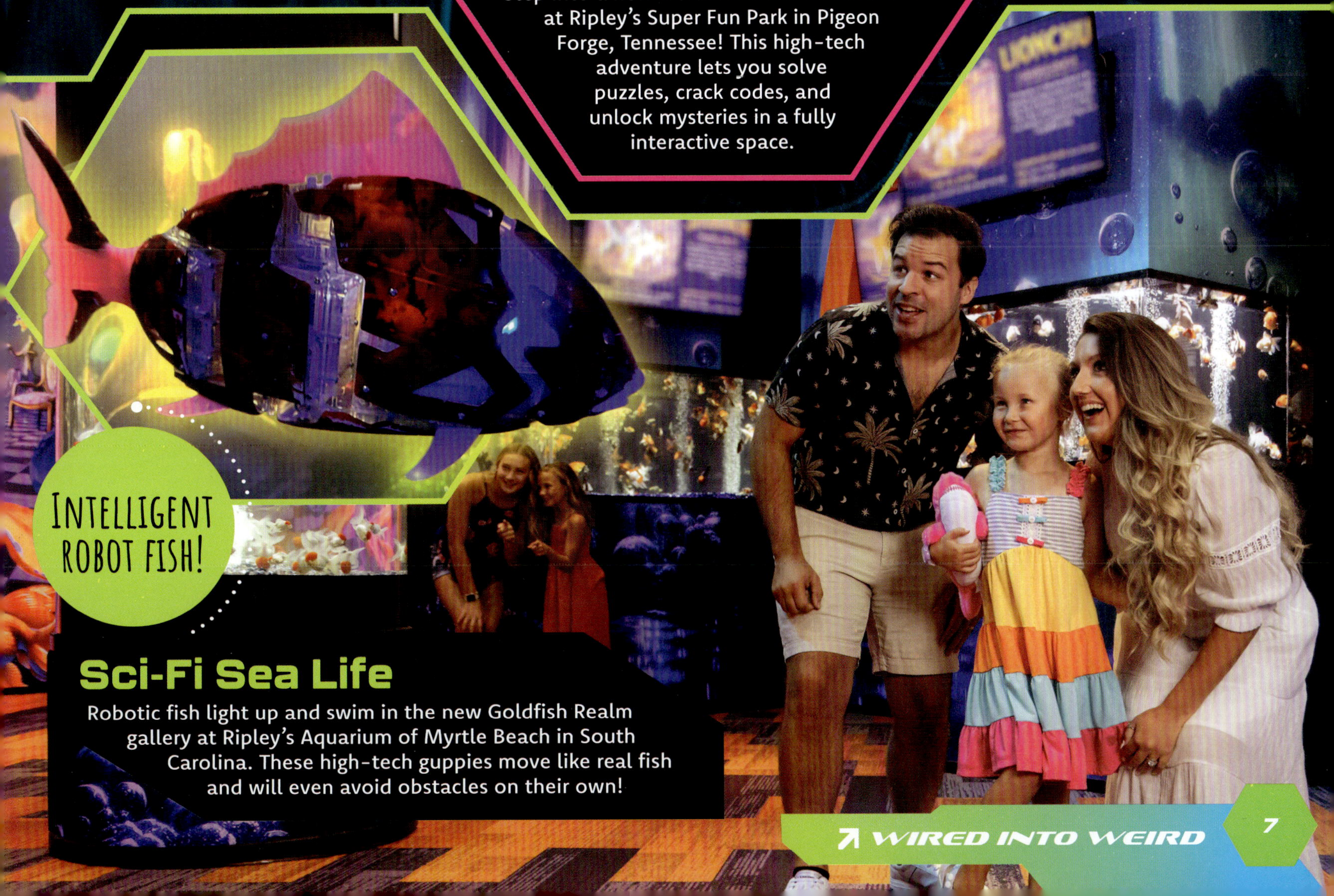

INTELLIGENT ROBOT FISH!

Sci-Fi Sea Life

Robotic fish light up and swim in the new Goldfish Realm gallery at Ripley's Aquarium of Myrtle Beach in South Carolina. These high-tech guppies move like real fish and will even avoid obstacles on their own!

THE ORIGINAL "Florida Man"

In 2025, Robert Ripley was honored in a big way with his induction into the Florida Tourism Hall of Fame.

Ripley helped shape Florida's strange and bold spirit, long before "Florida Man" was a thing. He even owned a home in the state. In 1940, he made history at Marineland with the world's first live underwater radio show, talking while feeding sharks. He even tried "milking" a rattlesnake! Ripley's fearless stunts helped build a wild legacy that still lives on in Florida today. In fact, the world headquarters of Ripley's Believe It or Not! is in Orlando.

TOURISM HALL OF FAME MEMBER!

RIPLEY'S POPULARITY GREW WITH EACH UNIQUE BROADCAST!

RIPLEY WITH SHARKS DURING THE WORLD'S FIRST LIVE UNDERWATER RADIO SHOW!

St. Augustine's Anniversary

In 2025, Ripley's Believe It or Not! in St. Augustine, Florida, celebrated 75 years as the very first and oldest permanent Ripley's Attraction in the word! It is inside Castle Warden, a historic building from 1887 where Ripley himself stayed several times in the 1940s. Since opening in 1950, it has amazed visitors with strange artifacts, jaw-dropping exhibits, and unforgettable experiences.

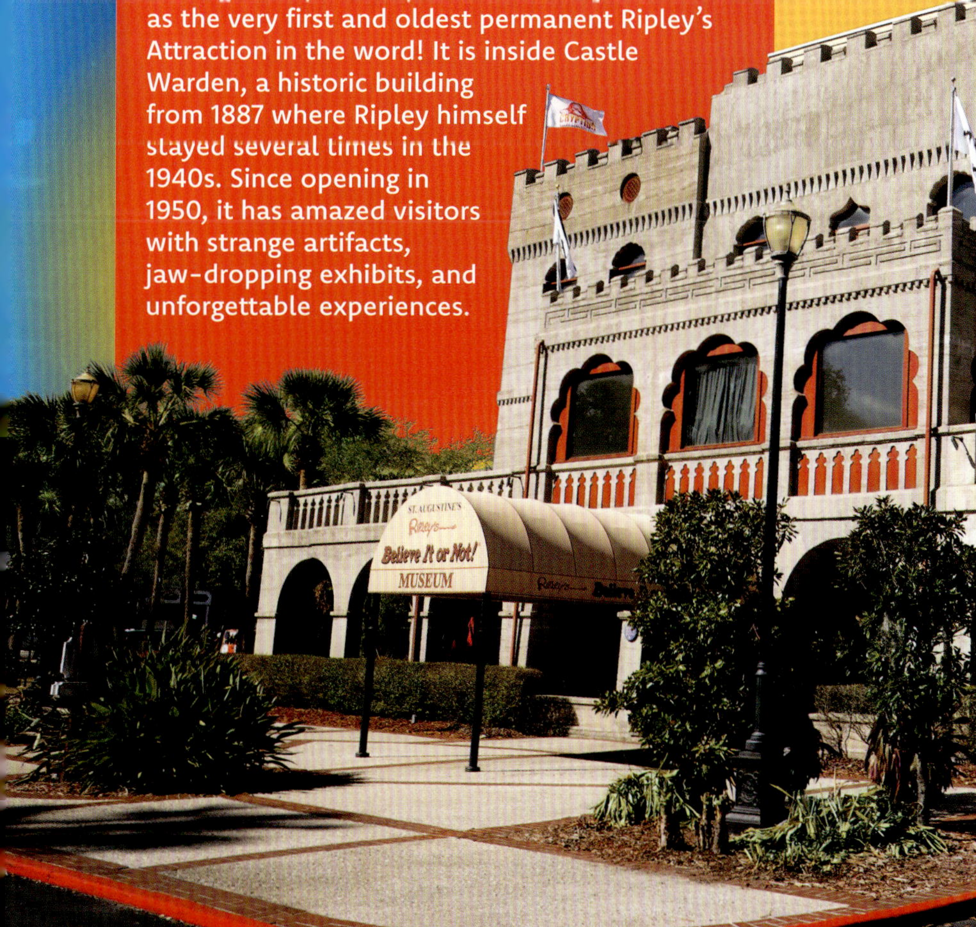

RIPLEY'S Believe It or Not! ST. AUGUSTINE 1950 2025 CELEBRATING 75 YEARS

Ripley's Believe It or Not! St. Augustine in the 1950s.

Latest Updates

Check out what's new from this past year at Ripley's Believe It or Not! World Entertainment!

1. A new **Ripley's Illusion Lab** location opened in Pigeon Forge, Tennessee.
2. **Julia Moellmann** won the company-wide Crazy Curator Contest with her exhibit ideas, earning her this shout-out and a genuine **two-headed cow** taxidermy!
3. A trio of **Hawaiian Falls** water parks in Texas joined the Ripley's Attractions family.
4. **Tommy Bartlett Exploratory** in Wisconsin Dells became part of Ripley's Attractions.
5. **Ripley's Aquarium of the Smokies** celebrated **25 years** since opening its doors in Gatlinburg, Tennessee.
6. The latest **Ripley's Crazy Golf** debuted in Orlando, Florida.
7. The **Ripley's Art Department** unveiled lifelike wax figures of actress and singer **Selena Gomez** and chef **Gordon Ramsay**.

TOMMY BARTLETT
EXPLORATORY
INTERACTIVE SCIENCE CENTER
4
5
25
RIPLEY'S
AQUARIUM
OF THE SMOKIES
RIPLEY'S
CRAZY
GOLF
6
7

WIRED
INTO
WE

IRD

UP NEXT...

BELIEVE
IT

CRASH COURSE

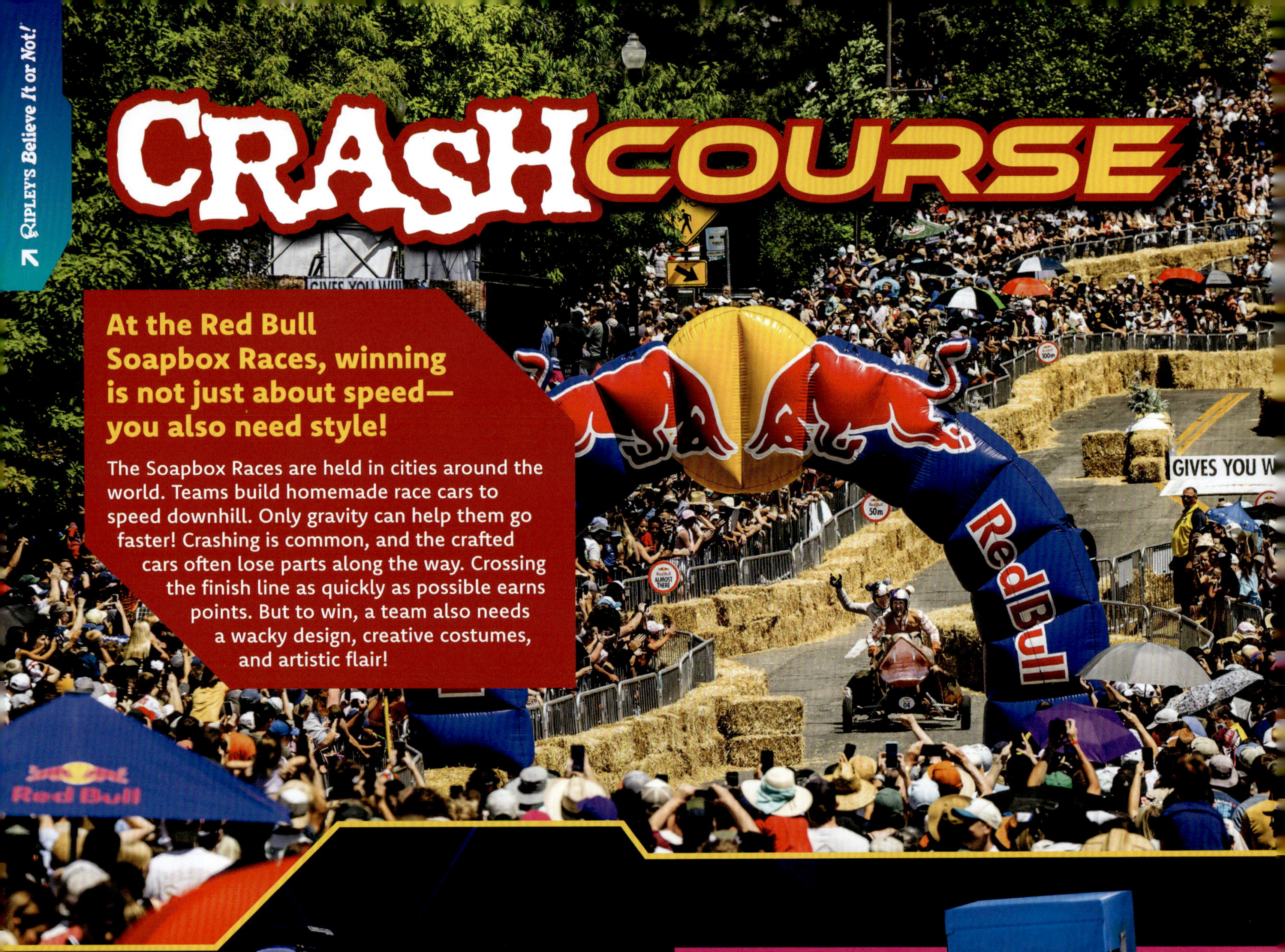

At the Red Bull Soapbox Races, winning is not just about speed—you also need style!

The Soapbox Races are held in cities around the world. Teams build homemade race cars to speed downhill. Only gravity can help them go faster! Crashing is common, and the crafted cars often lose parts along the way. Crossing the finish line as quickly as possible earns points. But to win, a team also needs a wacky design, creative costumes, and artistic flair!

Now that's fast food!

Edible Arrangements

Some musicians can make music from anything—including vegetables!

The London Vegetable Orchestra (LVO) carve their own instruments out of things like carrots, squashes, potatoes, peppers, and zucchinis. It was started by Tim Cranmore, who makes recorders. A friend challenged him to make one out of a carrot. And he did it! He teamed up with some students from the Royal Academy of Music in 2010 and formed the LVO. They have since traveled the world performing their vege-*tunes*. They've even jammed out at Windsor Castle with King Charles III!

The LVO performing in a Morrisons grocery store, which supplied the ensemble's vegetables for summer 2025.

Floating Fungi

Sam Shoemaker paddled across the ocean in a boat made from mushrooms! He grew the kayak himself in Los Angeles, California. Sam let it form naturally inside a kayak-shaped mold over six weeks. Then he let it dry out for three months. The 107-pound (48.5-kg) mushroom kayak carried him 26 miles (41.8 km) to San Pedro. The 12-hour trip certainly proved fungi can float. Sam even had a friendly fin whale follow him for a few miles of the journey!

NOT MUCH ROOM IN THIS MUSHROOM!

A ROYAL JAM SESSION!

MOUTH BACTERIA ↗ There are more bacteria living in your mouth than there are people living on the planet. The average human mouth can support up to 100 billion bacteria—more than 12 times the world population.

POTATO PERFUME ↗ A new perfume launched in 2024, called Polish Potatoes. It was inspired by perfumier Michal Gilbert Lach's childhood trips in the 1980s to vegetable markets in Poland.

LARGE FAMILY ↗ In 2025, Mzee Ernesto Muinuchi Kapinga from Tanzania had 16 wives, 104 children, and 144 grandchildren. He first married in 1961 and has a house for each of his wives.

CHEESE NACHOS ↗ Washington Capitals hockey goalie Logan Thompson was distracted from saving a shot by nachos. A spectator had thrown a tray of cheese-covered nachos onto the ice! Although the Edmonton Oilers' Corey Perry skated over the nachos to score, the Capitals still went on to win 3–2.

SNAKE ROBBERY ↗ Four people robbed a Tennessee convenience store armed with two pythons! They waved the snakes around as weapons and placed them on the counter to threaten and distract the clerks.

Fruit on Foot

Israeli athlete Moshe Lederfien has run more than 40 marathons with fruit balanced on his head! A marathon is 26.2 miles (42.2 km) long. In 2019 he completed 11 marathons balancing a pineapple on his head. In another race, Moshe swapped out the pineapple with a flowerpot! His next plan is to try balancing a watermelon.

JANUARY 7 ↗ NATIONAL BOBBLEHEAD DAY

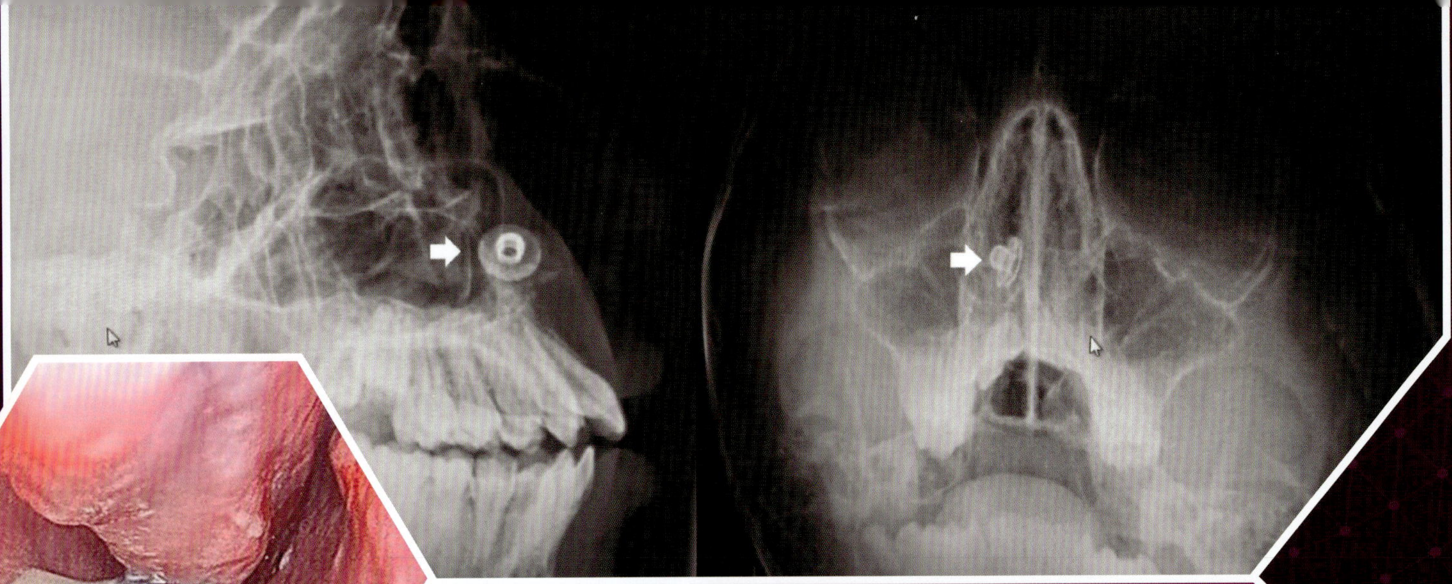

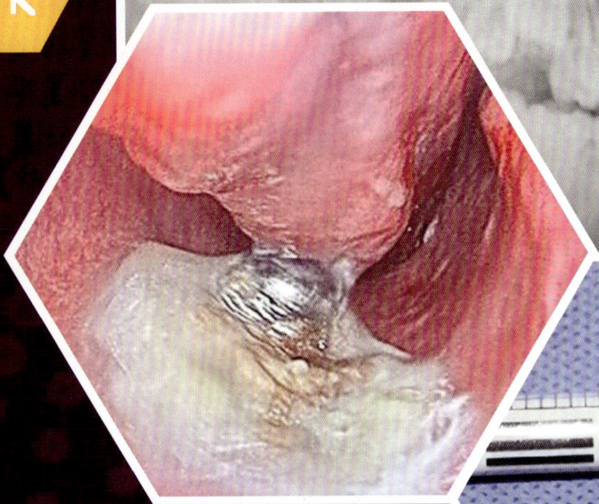

Booger Button

A teenager was shocked to discover an old metal button stuck up his nose—and it had been there for about 10 years! During a routine dental scan, a small button was spotted lodged in his nose. It was covered in mucus and crusty stuff. Eww! Luckily, the button was easy to remove with a small procedure. With the area numbed, the teenager simply had to sit up during the removal so as not to cause any damage to the area.

FAST LEARNER For the 1997 movie *Alien: Resurrection*, actress Sigourney Weaver had to perform a behind-the-back, half-court basketball shot. She made it after several takes and a few weeks of tutoring.

CLOSET RECORDING When American songwriter Charlie Puth asked Selena Gomez to sing on his composition "We Don't Talk Anymore," she recorded her vocals in his closet.

TOUPEE TRICK In February 2025, police officers at Rafael Nunez International Airport in Colombia arrested a 40-year-old man. He was attempting to smuggle illegal goods—worth about $10,000—out of the country under his toupee!

GAMING MARATHON Justin O'Donnell played the video game *World of Warcraft* for 78 hours 30 minutes straight in New Brunswick, New Jersey. It meant that he didn't sleep for more than three days.

Canine Conga

Thomas Lacey, from Germany, taught 11 dogs to dance in a conga line together! The animal trainer puts on *paw*-some stage shows with his canine costars. In their quirky act, the dogs perform all sorts of tricks and stunts to get a laugh! Believe it or not, before training dogs, Thomas worked with lions! He gets his love for animal training from his family, who have been training for generations.

SHAKE YOUR TAIL AND DO THE CONGA!

TAKING COVER

Nancy 3. Hoffman runs a museum on Peaks Island, Maine, that's all about umbrella covers!

The Umbrella Cover Museum started in 1996 as a collection of around 80 covers in Nancy 3.'s kitchen. After six years and many more covers, the museum was moved into a larger space. Today, the quirky collection now has more than 2,000 covers from 71 countries. Visitors can enjoy a tour from Nancy 3. herself, as well as a performance of the museum's theme song, "Let a Smile Be Your Umbrella (On a Rainy Day)."

NANCY ENTERTAINS GUESTS!

FAMILY LINK ↗ In a Harry Potter movie, English actor Hero Fiennes Tiffin played the younger version of his real-life uncle. Tiffin played 11-year-old Tom Riddle, the young Voldemort, in *Harry Potter and the Half-Blood Prince*. The adult Voldemort was played by his uncle, Ralph Fiennes.

220,000 DOTS ↗ French artist Georges Seurat painted by putting thousands of small dots of paint on the canvas. The technique is called pointillism. His 1886 painting *A Sunday on the Island of La Grande Jatte* is made up of around 220,000 individual dots.

TOXIC MAKEUP ↗ After catching smallpox in 1562, Queen Elizabeth I of England covered the scars on her face with homemade makeup. It was made from a highly toxic mixture of vinegar and lead.

SWALLOWING SICKNESS ↗ Elise Baynard from England has a very rare swallowing condition called achalasia. It means she has to stand while eating or drinking to avoid choking. Before her diagnosis, she regurgitated food and drink up to 60 times a day.

FATEFUL SONG ↗ The cruise liner *Costa Concordia* crashed into rocks and partially sank off the coast of Italy in 2012. When the collision occurred, a familiar song was playing in one of the ship's restaurants. It was Celine Dion's "My Heart Will Go On" from the movie *Titanic*!

SALTY STYLES

Artist Sigalit Landau makes art using the salty water of the Dead Sea!

She creates sculptures by leaving her chosen items, from ballet dresses to barbed wire, underwater. The Dead Sea has more salt in its water than any other ocean. Layers of salt slowly form on her pieces. The result? Each item is transformed. They look like they've been covered in sparkling crystals! One dress was even submerged for two years! Sigalit views the sea as her laboratory. Even though she has been experimenting for more than 20 years, she never quite knows how each piece will turn out.

Chili Desert

In fall, parts of the golden Gobi Desert turn red—with chilis! September and October are harvest months for chili farmers. After they've picked more than 200 tons of the bright-red fruits, they lay them out on the sand. It looks like a sea of red, stretching as far as the eye can see. The warm sunshine dries out the fruits in just a few weeks, ready to be sold.

CHILI HARVEST FROM ABOVE!

Scrapple is a traditional mix of pork scraps and cornmeal found in Pennsylvania and surrounding states.

Scrap Sculptures

At the Scrapple Sculpting Contest in Philadelphia, artists are given 90 minutes to show off their carving skills on a 5-pound (2.3-kg) hunk of meat mush called scrapple. With clay tools, knives, and their hands, they work hard and fast. The result? Fun creations that celebrate all things Philly. Past entries have included the Philadelphia Flyers' mascot "Gritty" and a miniature version of the Philadelphia Museum of Art's Rocky statue.

SNORKEL SPORT

What kind of game needs two teams, a heavy ball, and snorkels? Underwater rugby, of course!

Underwater rugby began in 1961 in Germany. It was used as a game to improve fitness. It's now played by countries across the world, including the U.S., China, and Mexico. Games last for 30 minutes. Each team has six players in the pool and six players on the side. The players wear masks, fins, snorkels, and mouth guards. The ball is negatively buoyant, which means it's full of water to stop it from floating to the water's surface. The aim of the game is to get the ball into the opponent's goal—a basket at the very bottom of the pool—while holding your breath!

Leap of Faith

Every February 6 in Andavías, Spain, women of all ages jump over a bonfire for Salto del Piorno! The youngest women are the first to jump. It is a tradition that has passed from mother to daughter for hundreds of years. They wear traditional dresses that can weigh up to 44 pounds (20 kg)! They roll up the fabric to stop it catching on fire. Salto del Piorno is in honor of Saint Agatha. It is believed that she prevents fires and has stopped Mount Etna from erupting.

Sandy Canvas

With just a rake, Pierre-Louis Cullier creates stunning art in the sand of France's Atlantic coast. The French artist always loved drawing and going to the beach, so he merged the two! Pierre-Louis can create a piece of art in just a few hours. He has designed sand pictures of a turtle, a tiger, and even a flying butterfly. Some almost look like a photograph! Beachgoers often stop to watch his strokes in the sand come to life.

HIDING PLACE ↗ Fugitive Deario Wilkerson tried to hide from police officers in the attic of a home in Memphis, Tennessee. But he literally fell into their laps when the attic floor collapsed beneath him and dropped him into the kitchen.

ENDURANCE DANCING ↗ In the 1920s and 1930s, endurance dance marathons in the United States could last up to five months! Competitors danced nonstop all that time, apart from pausing to rest for 15 minutes every hour. They even danced while they ate.

FOX TOOTH ↗ *Bald's Leechbook*, a medical textbook from the ninth–tenth century, has an interesting cure for swellings. It suggests removing a tooth from a live fox, wrapping the tooth in the skin of a deer fawn, and then placing the skin on the swollen area.

RAINBOW RUFFLES

Pet stylist Brigit Gross from Florida dyed her chicken's feathers the colors of the rainbow!

The hen, named McChicken, seemed to be more popular with her coop mates after her makeover. It might be because chickens have enhanced vision. Brigit has dyed other animal furs and feathers, too. Dogs, cats, ducks, and even a horse have visited her salon! She only ever uses animal-safe dye on her models. They always leave looking like they rule the roost!

WORD PLAY ↗ King Louis XIII of France, who ruled from 1610 to 1643, appointed a Royal Anagrammatist, Thomas Billon. He entertained the court by creating anagrams of people's names.

GHOSTLY CRIES ↗ Liu Chuanyi spent three days and nights trapped down a well without food or water. He had fallen to the bottom of a 39.4-foot-deep (12-m) well on the border between Thailand and Myanmar. Local villagers warily notified police after hearing his screams and mistaking them for ghost sounds.

LAUGHTER LAW ↗ In 2024, Japan's Yamagata prefecture passed an ordinance encouraging residents to laugh at least once a day. This was to promote good physical and mental health.

MOUNTAIN ANCESTOR ↗ The 8,261-foot-high (2,518-m) Mount Taranaki in New Zealand is legally recognized as a person. Indigenous Māori tribes have long considered the mountain to be an ancestor.

Vintage Meme

Funny cat pictures went "viral" long before the internet! In 1951, Nipper the cat appeared in newspapers across the United States for his love of eating corn on the cob. He liked it best covered in butter! His owner, Dorothy Brinn of Los Angeles, made him a special holder to keep the cob steady. Nipper enjoyed his treat so much that he ate about two ears of corn every day!

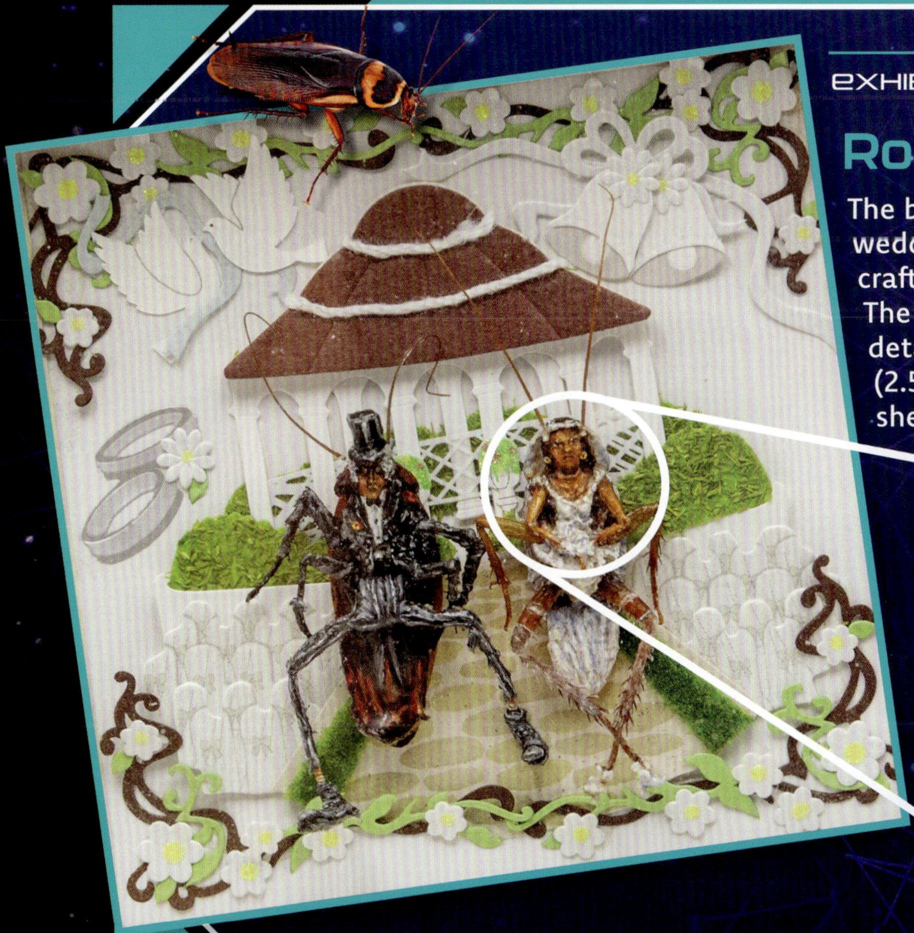

EXHIBIT NO. 167233

Roach Wedding

The bride and groom in this charming wedding scene are two cockroaches! It was crafted by Mexican artist Enrique Ramos. The insects are painted with amazing detail, despite being only about 1 inch (2.5 cm) long. You can even see the bride's sheer stockings on her hairy roach legs!

SEE MORE!

RIPLEY'S COLLECTION

BELIEVE IT

Nature WALK

Too many animals were being hit by cars on the Trans-Canada Highway in Banff National Park . . . so they built animal crossings!

Six of the crossings are overpasses that go over the road. They look just like normal bridges to drivers, but they're covered in trees and plants. Now animals like wolves, elk, and bears can cross from one side to another safely. In fact, there are now 80 percent fewer collisions!

I'M TAKING THE OVERPASS NEXT TIME!

Horse Power

When times get tough, people get creative. During World War II, the Netherlands faced a fuel shortage. Rather than let their car sit and gather dust, some people turned it into a horse-drawn carriage! By removing the engine, they reduced the car's weight and made space for a driver's seat. A few more modifications later—including adding a harness for the horse—and the car was road-ready once more!

MICRO CAMERA ↗ The OmniVision OVM6948 is a medical camera that measures only 0.03 × 0.03 × 0.05 inches (0.76 × 0.76 × 1.27 mm), making it about the size of a grain of sand.

JACKPOT DOUBLE ↗ Christine Wilson from Massachusetts won the $1 million state lottery jackpot twice in 10 weeks in 2024.

TEA PARTY ↗ During the Boston Tea Party of 1773, protestors dumped more than 92,000 pounds (41,730.5 kg) of tea into Boston Harbor—enough to fill 18.5 million teabags.

GREAT GRIP ↗ Early basketball games were played with soccer balls. Players used to rub coal dust on their hands to help them grip the ball better.

DIFFERENT YEARS ↗ Eve and Billy Humphrey of New Jersey welcomed twins who were born on different days and in different years. Baby Ezra was born at a hospital in Voorhees at 11:48 p.m. on December 31, 2023, and his twin brother Ezekiel was delivered at 12:28 a.m. on January 1, 2024.

DEAR DENTURES ↗ In 2024, a set of gold-mounted upper dentures worn by former British prime minister Sir Winston Churchill sold for more than $23,000.

FAMILY NAME ↗ Marie Antoinette, the wife of King Louis XVI of France, had 10 sisters, all called Maria.

LONG GAME

Modern lacrosse descends from a seventeenth-century game played by Native Americans that often lasted for several days, had as many as 1,000 players on each team, and took place on a field with goals up to several miles apart.

ELASTIC QUEST

"Ever since I can remember . . . I've had this quirky fascination with things that are round.

3,780 POUNDS (1,714.6 KG)! HEAVIER THAN A CAR!

RIPLEY'S EXCLUSIVE

Benji Williams of Arizona wants to create the world's largest rubber band ball!

He first began making the elastic balls when he was only six. Benji even visited the Ripley's warehouse in 2011 to see the world's biggest rubber band ball. He has spent 18 years slowly adding to his ball and has documented his progress along the way. It now weighs 3,780 pounds (1,714.6 kg)—more than his car! For Benji to capture the title, his rubber band ball will need to weigh over 9,400 pounds (4,263.8 kg). Ripley's caught up with Benji to check in on his progress.

Q: What sparked your interest in creating rubber band balls?

A: When I was six years old, my first-grade teacher pulled out a rubber band ball from her desk and started bouncing it. I wanted to make my own—but much bigger. At that point, I was hooked and my hobby was set. I have been adding to the ball ever since.

Q: What are some challenges you face when adding to the ball?

A: Putting rubber bands on the ball is hard because of how big it is. I use an office chair to help hold the rubber band while I pull it over the ball. Without the chair or help from another person, there is no way for me to put the rubber band on without it slipping off.

Benji has also made balls out of materials like paint, hot glue, aluminum foil, tape, yarn, plastic wrap, dirt, metal wire, balloons, and tinsel.

942 POUNDS (427.3 KG)!

In 2011, Benji visited the Ripley's warehouse in Orlando to see the current record holder for largest rubber band ball.

Ripley's Believe It or Not! www.ripleybooks.com 141
Feats
Ripley's REVISITED
Benji Williams
Joel Wahl
YOUR UPLOADS
www.ripleys.com/submit
Benji Williams of Los Angeles, California, has been making rubber-band balls since he was six. He went to Orlando, Florida, on vacation to visit Ripley's warehouse to see the world's biggest rubber-band ball, made by Joel Waul and weighing 9,432 lb (4,282 kg). Benji's ball is already well over 100 lb (45 kg)—and growing fast.

1,255 POUNDS (555.7 KG)!

Q: What makes the perfect rubber band?

A: A good rubber band has no seam lines and is not glued together. It needs to be a continuous loop with no lines or any surface marks on it.

Q: How often does a band break?

A: The rubber bands I use rarely break. I usually check the rubber band to make sure it does not have any weak spots before placing it.

Q: Beyond beating the record, how big do you want your rubber band ball to get?

A: I would like to get the ball to roughly 22,000 pounds (9,979 kg).

Q: What do you plan to do with the rubber band ball when it's complete?

A: My rubber band ball represents my entire life legacy. To be honest, I have never given any thought to what I would do when I am finished with it or if I will ever be finished.

CLOSE ENCOUNTERS

Imagine looking out of your window and seeing icebergs 10 times the height of your house! It's *snow* joke!

This happened in July 2025 in Innaarsuit, Greenland. Colossal icebergs came so close to land, they cast shadows over the coastal town. Some people were worried, but some were excited! Warnings were put out, asking people to keep away. The emergency services closed the fish factory and stores on the harbor. It was unlikely that chunks of ice would have fallen onto the land. But if they had crashed into the water, they might have caused waves that flooded the town! In the end, the icebergs just drifted away.

THOSE ARE SOME BIG BERGS!

Martian Millions

In 2025, a meteorite from Mars sold at auction for $5.3 million! The space rock is officially known as NWA 16788. It is reddish in color, just like the planet. It also has a scorched outer layer from traveling through Earth's atmosphere. The out-of-this-world find was discovered in the Sahara by a meteorite hunter in 2023. It weighs 54 pounds (24.5 kg), making it the largest piece of Mars ever found on Earth!

GRINCH STOLEN ↗ A curious bear stole an inflatable Grinch Christmas decoration from the yard of Shanick Suarez's home in Naples, Florida. The bear dragged the Grinch off into some nearby woods. It was later recovered but was beyond repair.

CLEVER PARROT ↗ Apollo, an African gray parrot belonging to Dalton and Tori Mason from Florida, has more than 4.4 million followers on social media. He has the intelligence of a human toddler. He knows all the basic colors, can identify numerous different objects, and can ask and answer questions in English.

FREE LABOR ↗ A family of beavers took a couple of days to build a dam that the Czech Republic government had been planning for seven years. The project to build a dam at the Brdy Nature Park began in 2018 but had been constantly delayed. It would have cost over $1.2 million, but the beavers did it for free.

ANGRY BIRDS ↗ Crows can remember people's faces for many years. They associate human faces with either danger or friendliness and will hold grudges for long periods. They even tell other crows about people they have met. So never annoy a crow!

Titan Telescope

Nestled in the mountains of China, there's a giant telescope that's as wide as five football fields! It would take about two hours to walk all the way around it. It's called the Five-hundred-meter Aperture Spherical Telescope, or FAST. Astronomers started using the telescope in 2020 to study space. It has over 4,000 panels that can be adjusted for each test. It is so powerful that it will be used to make a clear map of the Milky Way galaxy and beyond!

FAN SHARE

Lemon Legend

Back in 1978, Ripley's Believe It or Not! published a story in our daily cartoon about a lemon that had been preserved for 32 years! In 1946, it was put into the duffel bag of Ralph Pierson. Now the lemon and its legend are being passed down from generation to generation. Judy Lemke from Des Moines, Washington State, got in touch to tell us that she is the latest lucky keeper. And although it is a bit dark in color, the lemon is still going strong!

SHARE YOUR STORY AT
RIPLEYS.COM/SHARE

MANY MARATHONS In 2024, Steve Edwards from Gloucestershire, England, completed his 1,000th full marathon—and he finished each one in under four hours. He ran his first marathon in 1981 at age 18 and has since run more than 26,200 miles (42,164.8 km)—further than the circumference of Earth.

BIG BIKE Frenchmen Nicolas Barrioz and David Peyrou spent two years building a rideable bicycle that measures a colossal 25.5 feet (7.8 m) high. The pedals are connected to the rear wheel by a 52.5-foot-long (16-m) chain. The bike even has a bell in case other road users don't see it coming!

52-DAY RACE The annual Sri Chinmoy Self-Transcendence 3100-Mile Race is one of the world's toughest sports events. Athletes try to complete 5,649 laps around a city block in Queens, New York City, in 52 days. They can run from 6:00 a.m. to midnight, averaging nearly 60 miles (96.6 km) a day.

Safety First

Billie Jean is a chicken who likes to go on a stroll, sometimes even crossing the road! To keep her safe, a few locals decided to put her in a reflective vest. She lives at the Railway Inn in Gloucestershire, England, but is often out and about. She once ended up a few miles away from her home! The whole town loves Billie Jean. She often follows people home and even walks with children on their way to school!

Juggling Joyride

Using a 13.1-foot (4-m) tube, Wes Peden turns his body into a juggling roller coaster!

Wes has been juggling since he was just five years old. The New Yorker was inspired by his dad—also a professional juggler. Wes mastered the art when he was young and has performed in more than 25 countries around the world! He loves to come up with new tricks and forms of juggling. In one of his shows, he zips a ball around in a long clear tube like a roller coaster. By swinging the tube and moving his body, he makes the ball zip from one side, out of the other, and back into the tube!

A JUGGLING SENSATION!

WITH HIS RINGS ALL IN A ROW!

PAPER THIN

Octopuses are a bizarre bunch, but the argonaut stands out by being the only kind that can make its own "shell!"

It's really an egg case, not a shell, though it sure looks like one! The thin case gives this animal its other name: paper nautilus. The female secretes the shell material from her arms. She starts to make it when she's just two weeks old. It is not attached to her body. Instead, she carries it around with her arms, ready to store her eggs. This shell can reach up to 12 inches (30.5 cm) long, which is about the same length as her body! Besides holding eggs, the argonaut can also fill her case with air to stop herself from sinking to the ocean floor.

Sky-High Sunflower

A sunflower in the Netherlands grew so tall that it needed its own scaffolding! Jeroen van der Velde has been growing sunflowers since he was a kid. In 2025, one of his prize blooms reached epic heights. It grew to 30.1 feet (9.2 m) tall! Jeroen had to build scaffolding to support the sunflower. It also allowed him to care for the plant, three times a day, without causing any damage. Jeroen is so committed that he doesn't go on vacation during sunflower season!

30.1 FEET (9.2 M) TALL!

Jeroen van der Velde

UPSIDE DOWN Whipnose anglerfish swim upside down while hunting. A long lure like a fishing line extends from the fish's head. This lure contains bacteria that glow in the dark. The fish's muscular system allows it to jerk the lure back and forth to attract prey. By swimming upside down, the fish can get closer to prey living on the ocean floor.

SHARK TRANCE You probably wouldn't want to tickle a shark. Especially a ferocious tiger shark. But these fearsome creatures can be put into a trance-like state called tonic immobility. It occurs when the sharks are gently turned on their back and rubbed on their ultra-sensitive snouts. If undisturbed, they can remain in a trance for 15 minutes.

LAST BIRDS The last known Carolina parakeet in the world named Incas died at the Cincinnati Zoo in 1918. And he died in the very same enclosure where the world's last passenger pigeon Martha had passed away four years earlier.

Argonauts are often seen hitching rides on top of jellyfish!

Empty shell

SNAKE INVASION ↗ Snake catcher Dylan Cooper removed 102 venomous snakes from the backyard of an Australian home. There were five adult red-bellied black snakes and 97 babies. They were found in a pile of garden mulch outside client David Stein's home in Sydney.

CAT WALK ↗ Family cat Rayne Beau ran off during a camping trip in Yellowstone National Park in Wyoming. Two months later, he turned up in Roseville, California, nearly 900 miles (1,448.4 km) away. He had lost a lot of weight, and his paws were sore. His owners, Benny and Susanne Anguiano, think he was trying to walk all the way back to their home in Salinas, which would have added an additional 200 miles (321.8 km) to his journey!

LEANING TREES ↗ Reaching up to 98.4 feet (30 m) tall, Cook pine trees grow leaning toward the equator. In the Northern Hemisphere they lean south, and in the Southern Hemisphere they lean north. Their average tilt is 8.5 degrees—double that of the Leaning Tower of Pisa. The further away from the equator they are, the greater the slant. One tree in South Australia has a 40-degree tilt.

RIPLEY'S COLLECTION

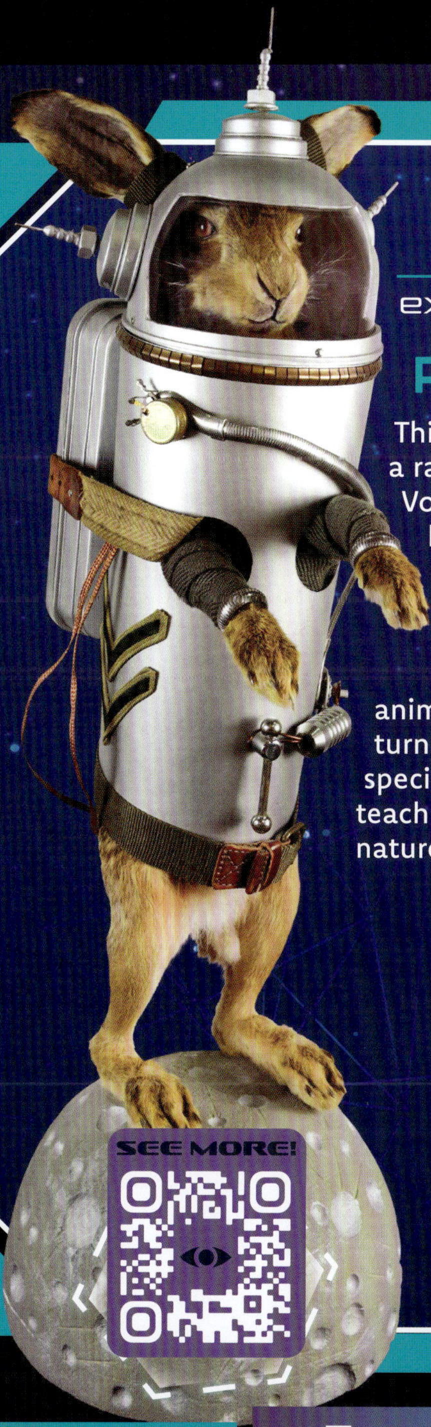

EXHIBIT NO. 171987

Rocket Rabbit

This quirky taxidermy of a rabbit is called "The Voyager." It was made by artist Lucia Mocnay. She lives in Australia, where rabbits are invasive. They can make it difficult for native animals to survive. Lucia turns the remains of invasive species like rabbits into art to teach people why balance in nature is important.

FACT FILES

An invasive species is not a natural part of an ecosystem. Someone brings in a few, and then they multiply.

BRICK Blooms

There was an unusual sight at Ireland's Bord Bia Bloom gardening show in 2025—flowers made of toy bricks!

The plastic blooms were the work of artist Gary Kirwan. He wanted to create something beautiful that anyone could also make. It took him more than eight weeks and more than 800,000 LEGO bricks. The balcony garden even had colorful planters for the walls and ground. Some of the brick flowers Gary made included tulips, daffodils, and sunflowers. He even mounted a brick birdhouse on the wall!

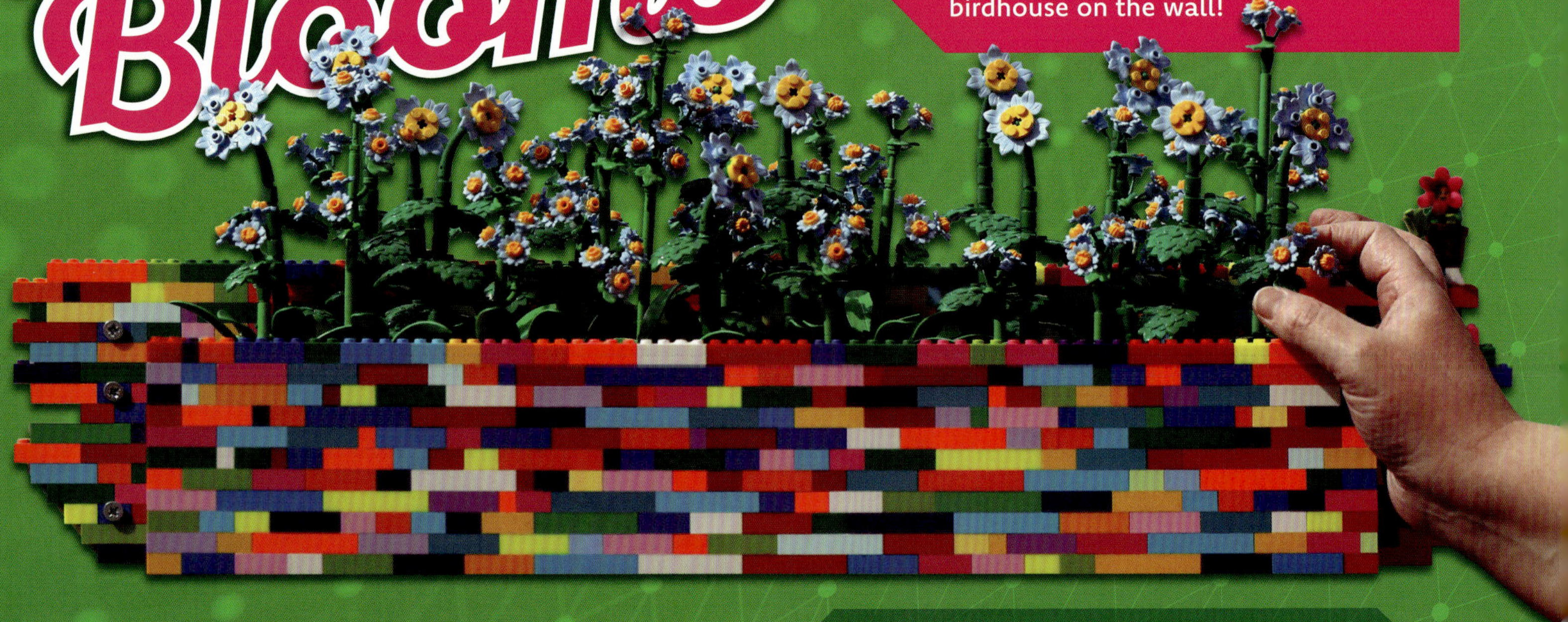

SUPER SURVIVOR ↗ While serving with the British Army in the Boer War, World War I, and World War II, Adrian Carton de Wiart survived being shot in the face, head, stomach, ankle, hip, leg, and ear—injuries that left him blind in one eye and missing part of an ear. In 1915, he lost his left hand, tearing off his own fingers when a doctor refused to amputate them. He also survived two plane crashes before eventually dying of natural causes at age 83.

MEDAL METAL ↗ Every medal at the 2024 Paris Olympics and Paralympics contained a piece of iron from the Eiffel Tower. The metal was taken from the monument's structure during renovation work in the twentieth century.

KIDNEY COLLECTION ↗ After experiencing a fever and pain in her lower back, Xiao Yu from Taiwan underwent surgery to remove more than 300 small stones from her right kidney.

BROKEN CHOPSTICKS ↗ When a man was admitted to a hospital in Dong Hoi, Vietnam, after complaining of severe headaches for five months and a weird discharge from his nose, a CT scan revealed that he had a pair of broken chopsticks embedded in his skull. Doctors performed surgery to remove the chopsticks, which had apparently been rammed up his nose during a brawl with such force that they had penetrated his brain.

Poppy Plane

Lithuanian artist Darius Sirmulevicius made a giant plane out of ceramic poppies! He made more than 20,000 of the red flowers by hand, each with a unique design. The display was in the shape of a Lancaster Bomber plane. It honored the pilots who lost their lives during World War II. For a few months in 2025, visitors could visit the display at the International Bomber Command Centre in Lincoln, UK. Then each handmade poppy was sold for around $50 to raise money for charity.

FACT FILES

Poppies are a symbol of remembrance in the UK.

Pretty Potholes

Harry Smith-Haggett, from the UK, started planting flowers in road potholes to make people notice them! His first pothole plant was just outside his house. He became fed up with the hole in the road. Just two days after adding the flowers, the hole was fixed. Someone had noticed! So Harry carried on. He wears a pink, high-visibility "Pretty Pot Holes" work vest. He has planted flowers in hundreds of potholes across the UK. Sometimes people send him road names and ask him to pretty up its potholes!

Floki's Flow

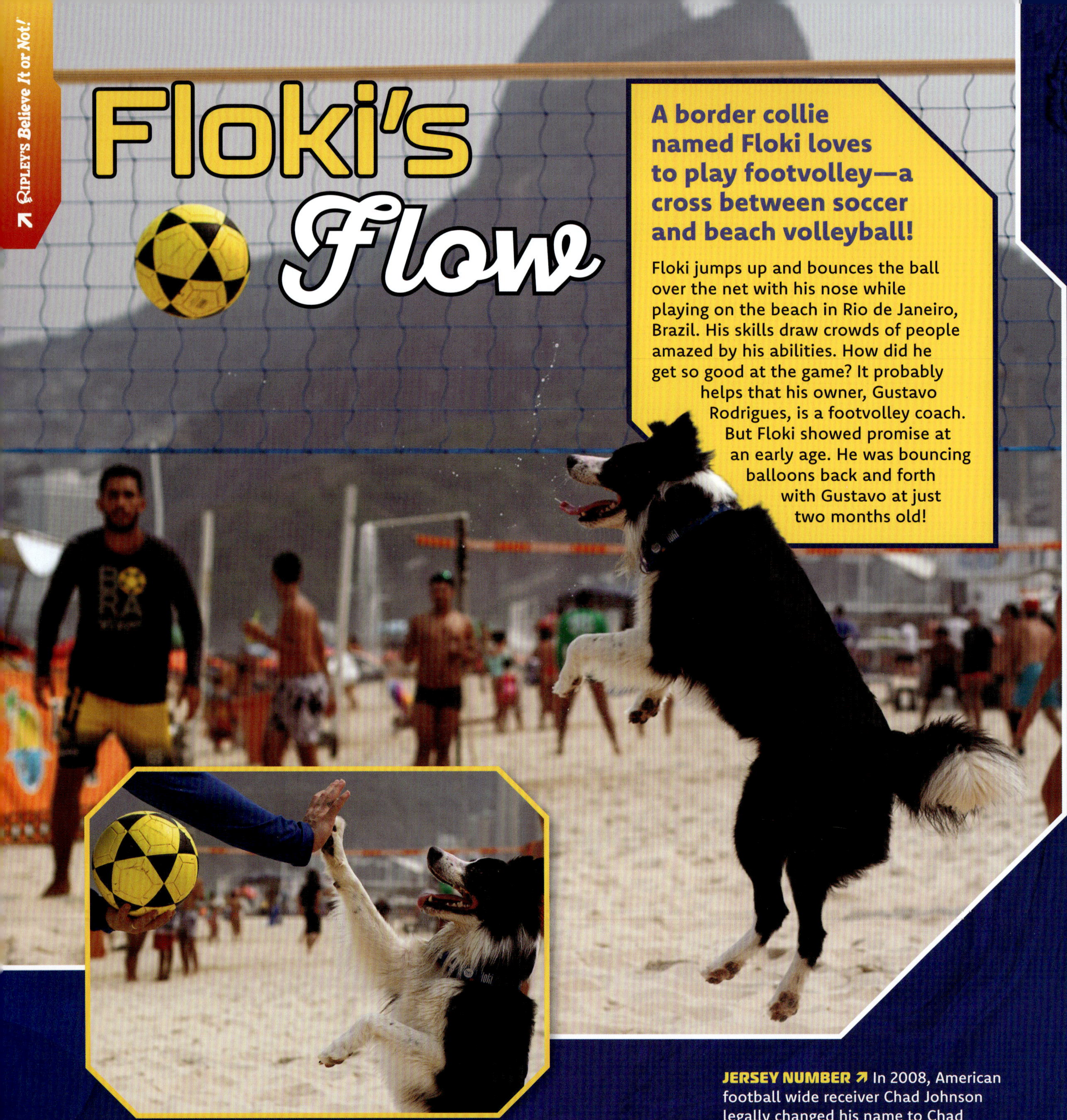

A border collie named Floki loves to play footvolley—a cross between soccer and beach volleyball!

Floki jumps up and bounces the ball over the net with his nose while playing on the beach in Rio de Janeiro, Brazil. His skills draw crowds of people amazed by his abilities. How did he get so good at the game? It probably helps that his owner, Gustavo Rodrigues, is a footvolley coach. But Floki showed promise at an early age. He was bouncing balloons back and forth with Gustavo at just two months old!

WEATHER GLITCH ↗ On October 10, 2024, a glitch on the BBC weather app led to catastrophic predictions for the UK. It forecast nighttime temperatures of over 752°F (400°C) and winds of 15,000 mph (24,140.2 kmph)!

SUNFISH SWEATER ↗ Japanese clothing brand Felissimo designed a sweater in the shape of a sunfish. Its fins acted as sleeves and its mouth as the collar.

CEILING SPACE ↗ Before 1834, women could only watch debates in the UK's parliament via a ceiling ventilation shaft. Women were banned from entering the chamber of the House of Commons, so they crept into the shaft instead. The roof space was originally created to take away the heat from the candles that lit the chamber. It was cramped and uncomfortable, and there was only room for 25 women at a time.

JERSEY NUMBER ↗ In 2008, American football wide receiver Chad Johnson legally changed his name to Chad Ochocinco. Ochocinco means "eight five" in Spanish, and 85 was his jersey number for the Cincinnati Bengals. He changed his name back to Johnson four years later.

LUCKY DAY ↗ Many people choose family birthdays as their lucky numbers when playing the lottery. But a woman in Maryland won $100,000 by purchasing tickets bearing the last five digits from her car's odometer.

Cycle Ball

The game of cycle ball doesn't need fancy footwork—just awesome wheel-work! The sport dates back more than 100 years. In it, players ride specialized bikes. They try to score (and save) goals using only their front and back wheels. The ball can fly at the goal at a powerful 43.5 mph (70 kmph)! The goalkeeper can use their hands—but no one can touch the floor!

Kicking Legend

Tom Dempsey was born with no toes on his right kicking foot and no fingers on his right hand, but he still became a pro football player! His dad encouraged him to focus on what he could do—not what he couldn't. And Tom did just that. In 1970, Tom kicked a 63-yard field goal to win a game for the New Orleans Saints. That kick was so amazing, it held a record for many years! Tom had a custom kicking shoe and played in the NFL for five teams over 11 seasons.

Lounge Landmark

A sofa dumped on the side of a road in Lydbrook, England, became a hot spot for photos! In April 2025, photographer Alex Elton-Wall started snapping pics of locals on the couch. Soon, other items started to show up by the sofa. At one point there was a window with curtains, a lamp, side tables, and even a houseplant! Alex took more than 140 portraits at “Lydbrook Lounge”—including of a horse, tortoise, and dogs—before it suddenly vanished.

Dad Games

Get ready for dad chaos! Fathers raced, tumbled, and tossed their way through Maryland's first-ever “Dad Games.” During the event, dads competed in a series of tasks. They dashed through the One-Trip Grocery Bag Relay, each carrying 15 shopping bags in just one trip! The dads also took on the Diaper Change Race and the Wiffle Ball Home Run Derby. Kids refereed most of the events, wearing black-and-white striped shirts and stopwatches around their necks.

STILT *Skater*

Figure skater Alisa Pilishenko from Ukraine glides across the ice on 20-inch-tall (50.8-cm) skates!

Alisa started figure skating when she was just four years old. She went on to be a competitive skater until she was 20. Alisa started performing in shows and tried using stilt skates for the first time in 2019. It took Alisa a lot of practice. The skates were tricky to master at first. She tried to walk and stand in them to get comfortable. Alisa now performs stunning routines, spinning and dancing without falling. She even twirls a fiery baton!

Completely CAPTIVATED

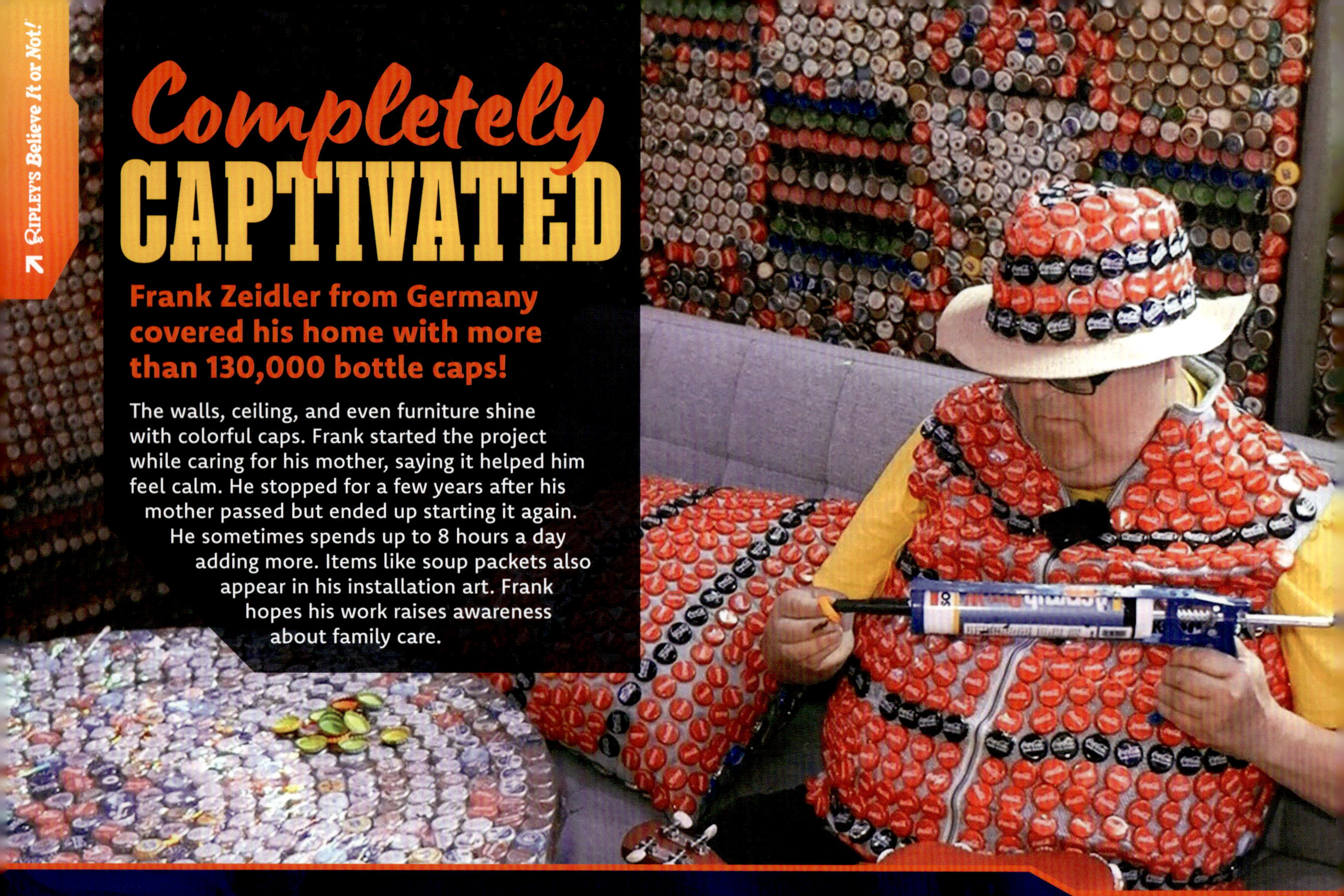

Frank Zeidler from Germany covered his home with more than 130,000 bottle caps!

The walls, ceiling, and even furniture shine with colorful caps. Frank started the project while caring for his mother, saying it helped him feel calm. He stopped for a few years after his mother passed but ended up starting it again. He sometimes spends up to 8 hours a day adding more. Items like soup packets also appear in his installation art. Frank hopes his work raises awareness about family care.

FAST FOOD AUTO-MATED SYSTEM!

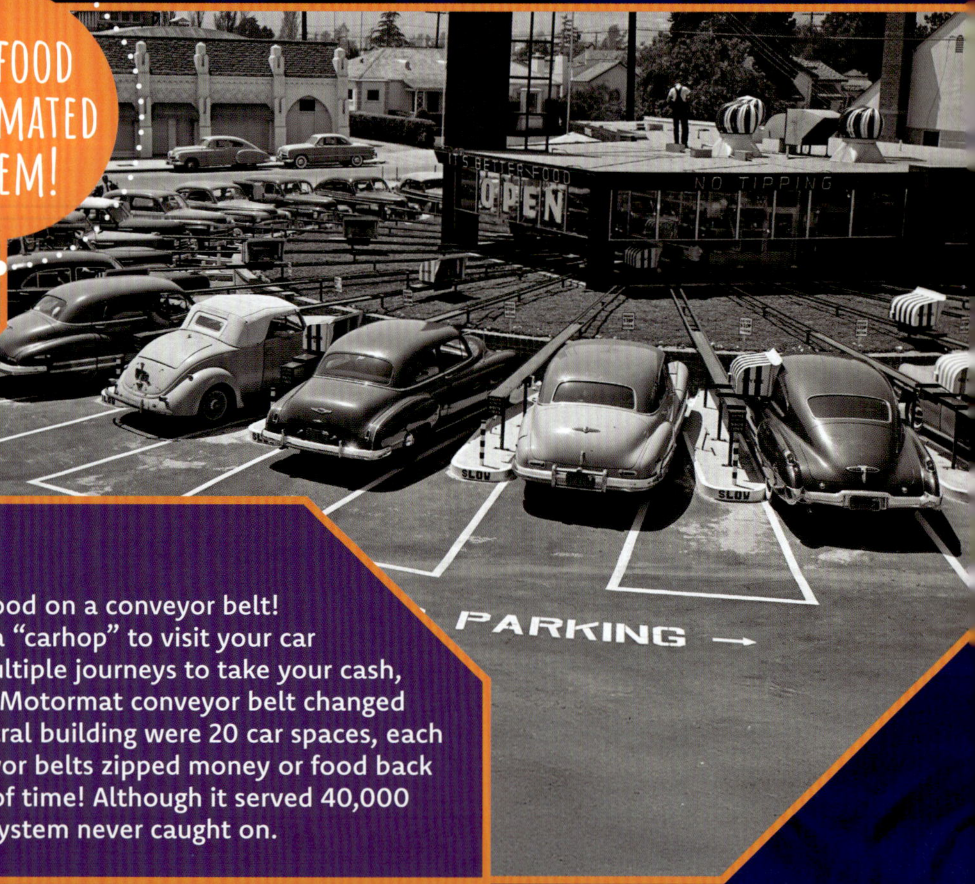

Faster Food

In 1949, a restaurant in Los Angeles served fast food on a conveyor belt! At that time, it was common for a waiter called a "carhop" to visit your car window to take your order. They'd then make multiple journeys to take your cash, deliver your change, and bring your food. The Motormat conveyor belt changed all that—for a while anyway. Around a central building were 20 car spaces, each next to a mini conveyor belt. The conveyor belts zipped money or food back and forth inside of a box, saving lots of time! Although it served 40,000 people in the first two weeks, the system never caught on.

BOTTLE CAPS COVER EVERY SURFACE!

Tricky Treat

Dondurma is ice cream that doesn't easily melt and can be eaten with a fork and knife! The Turkish dessert is dense and super stretchy. It gets its texture from salep, a flour made from powdered orchid bulbs. Street vendors use long metal rods to beat and knead the taffy-like ice cream. If you want to buy the treat, be ready for the vendors to play tricks on you. They might give you a scoop and then pretend to snatch it right out of your hands—just for fun!

EXHIBIT NO. 176283

Etch A Skeleton

Arist Jane Labowitch, also known as Princess Etch, drew a life-size skeleton using 11 different Etch A Sketches! Each piece shows a different part of the body, from ribs to hands to feet. Together the pieces form a skeleton made from the tiny, twist-and-turn screens.

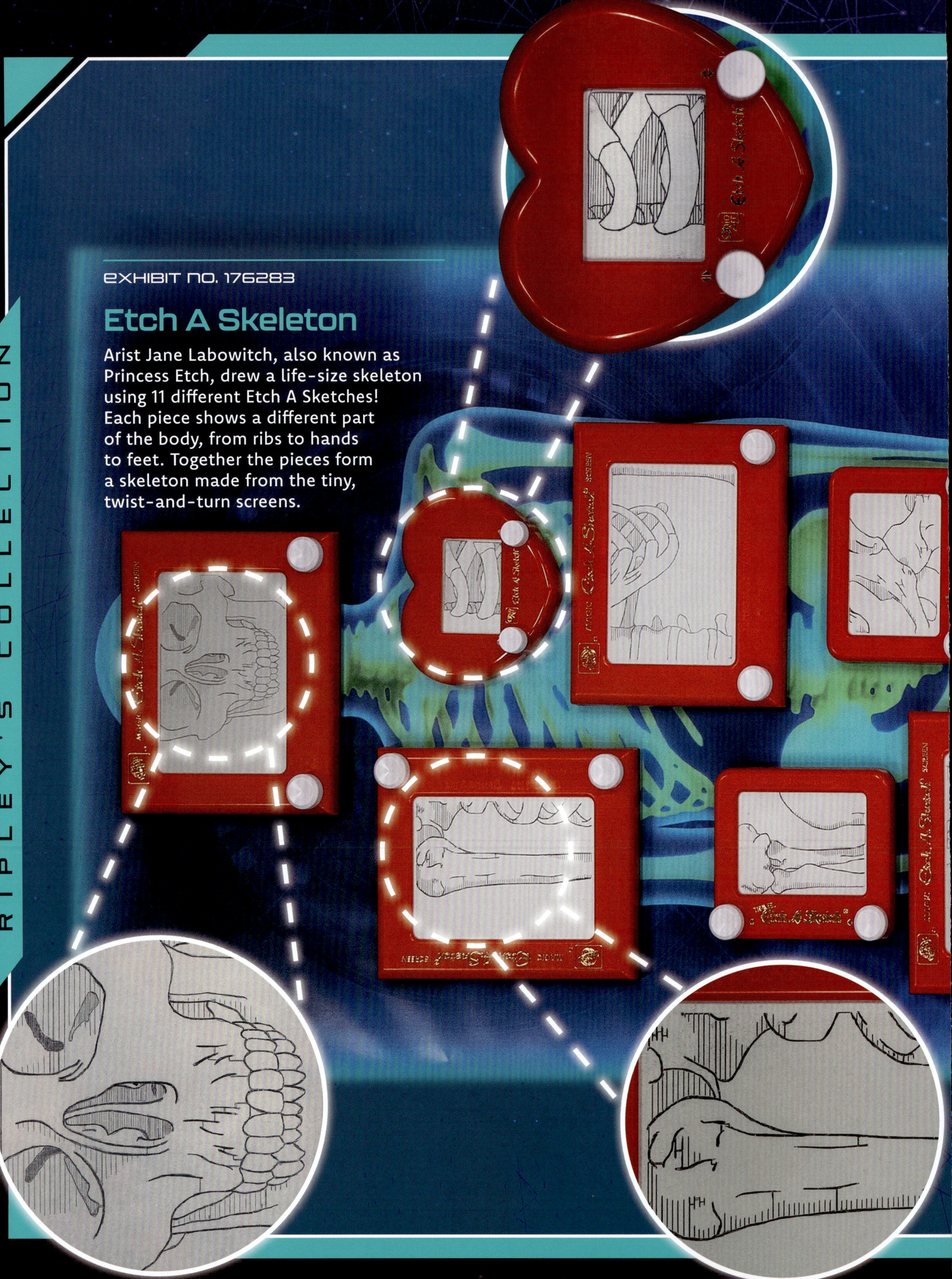

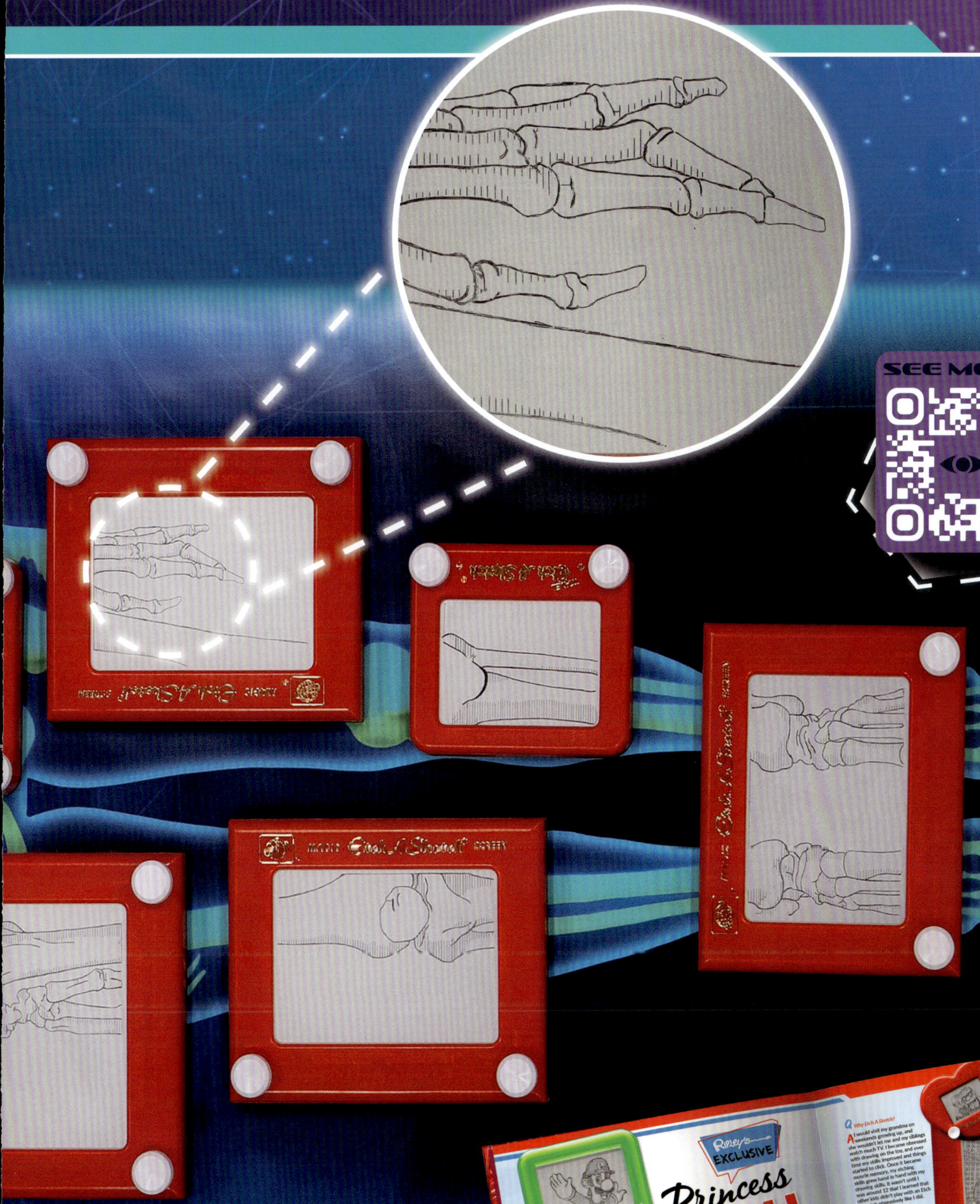

Ripley's EXCLUSIVE

Princess ETCH

Jane Labowitch of Chicago, Illinois, can create incredibly detailed drawings on Etch A Sketch toys!

Jane, aka Princess Etch, started playing with an Etch A Sketch at the age of four and now in her late twenties is a full-time etching artist. Invented in France more than 60 years ago, the Etch A Sketch works by turning knobs connected to a pulley system that drags a stylus along a clear screen coated with aluminum powder. The stylus removes the powder, drawing a line that shows the dark-colored inside of the toy. Shake the toy and the powder recoats the screen. It's simple, but not easy, so we reached out to Jane to ask her some questions about creating Etch A Sketch art.

Q Why Etch A Sketch?

A I would visit my grandma on weekends growing up, and she wouldn't let me and my siblings watch much TV. I became obsessed with drawing on the toy, and over time my skills improved and things started to click. Once it became muscle memory, my etching skills grew hand in hand with my drawing skills. It wasn't until I was around 12 that I learned that other kids didn't play with an Etch A Sketch obsessively like I did.

Q How do you keep your art from disappearing if someone shakes it?

A I drill a hole in the back of the Etch A Sketch and remove the excess aluminum powder from the inside. That way, when you shake the Etch A Sketch, there is nothing left to recoat the screen, and the image that is etched on the screen will remain intact. I then glue down the knobs so that they cannot be turned anymore. I've shipped my art all over the world and every rendition has safely arrived at its destination!

Q What happens if you make a mistake while sketching?

A If it's a small mistake, I can usually cover it up with shading or layering lines on top. If it's a medium mistake, I can tilt the Etch A Sketch and tap it from beneath, causing powder inside to recoat a portion of the screen. It's not an exact science and can cause much of the image to erase, but it's a good way to only remove a part of an etching. If the mistake is really bad, the easiest thing to do is shake the Etch A Sketch and start over! I try to etch the most difficult things first for that reason.

Q How many Etch A Sketches do you own?

A The number fluctuates, but at any given time I typically have at least 300!

Q What are some of your other interests?

A I love roller coasters! I worked at Cedar Point one summer because it's known for having some of the best coasters in the world. I also enjoy traveling, playing Uno, watching Frasier, and trying out macaroni and cheese at different restaurants.

Q Do you make any other kind of art?

A I do! I draw, paint watercolors, create digital illustrations, and love experimenting with different kinds of markers and pens.

Q Who are some artists you look up to?

A Some of my favorite traditional artists are Van Gogh, M. C. Escher, and Keith Haring. I am continually inspired by the small but vibrant community of Etch A Sketch artists, many of which have become my friends through our shared love of the medium. I also look up to my professors from college and peers who have taken different artistic paths since graduation.

Jane was featured in our 16th annual book, Ripley's Believe It or Not! Beyond the Bizarre! Since then, she has made many Etch A Sketch artworks for Ripley's.

UP NEXT...

INCREDIBLE PEOPLE

RIPLEY'S EXCLUSIVE

NERVES OF STEEL

Sideshow daredevil Auzzy Blood performs extreme stunts that leave audiences gasping!

One of his most jaw-dropping acts involves him threading a giant hook up his nose and out of his mouth—then hanging from it! Auzzy is also a talented sword swallower. He can swallow curved blades, serrated blades, weighted blades, multiple blades stacked together—you name it! He can even do clapping push-ups with a sword down his throat! Believe it or not, Auzzy taught himself how to do all these stunts and more. Auzzy sat down with Ripley's to dish the deets on his death-defying craft.

> “It's all about pushing the human body to give others an experience that they've never had before.

Q: What made you want to do these types of stunts?

A: Why not? Why not live an extraordinary life and have an adventure with my everyday life instead of living a normal nine-to-five, regular-person life?

Q: What does it feel like to swallow a sword?

A: The best way I can describe what it feels like is for you to imagine a long, solid piece of food that you can feel from the back of your throat all the way to your stomach. It's an insane feeling, and it's something you have to experience to understand.

Q: What does having a giant hook inside of your face feel like?

A: It's like I have a big hard booger that's metal, and I can feel it poking at the back of my throat. It's so strange because that's the best way I can describe it. It's literally like the hardest booger you have ever had, and it's just hooked into your face.

Pulling a truck with a sword down his throat!

Hanging from a hook in his face!

Q: How do people react when watching you perform?

A: Everything from gasping, screaming and squealing, running away. I've had people fainting, literally passing out. Online, with AI and developing technologies, it's hard to tell what is real and what is computer generated. But that gives me more of an edge. What I do becomes even more intense once people realize it's 100 percent real.

Q: How do you balance safety with extreme stunts? Have you ever been seriously hurt?

A: It's all about critical risk assessment. I try to analyze the situation as much as possible. I've had minor close calls and things that have almost sent me to the hospital, but I'm lucky that in my 10 years of performing I've never sustained an injury. I do some of the most dangerous things in sideshow history, and I've conditioned my mental space and my body to be able to do those things without getting injured.

DON'T TRY THIS AT HOME!

Made with Love

João Stanganelli Jr. of Brazil is on a mission to help every child to feel special—one doll at a time!

João has a condition called vitiligo. It causes his skin to lose color in patches. As a gift for his granddaughter to remember him by, he made a doll with vitiligo. She loved it, so João shared the doll online. Soon, people were asking him for dolls that celebrate their differences! He has since made around 200 custom dolls. Many have vitiligo, but he has also made dolls with alopecia, that use a wheelchair, and have a cochlear implant. João loves how happy his dolls make kids and plans to crochet them for as long as he can!

FACT FILES

Alopecia is a condition that causes bald spots. Cochlear implants are medical devices used by some people with severe hearing loss.

Cozy Country

A group of women knitted and crocheted a wool map of Ireland that is 12 × 11 feet (3.7 × 3.4 m)! The women live in County Wicklow, Ireland, and began the project in 2019. They would meet every Wednesday to brainstorm what landmarks needed to be added to the map. It's filled with cute little details, such as a small garden and a local dolphin named Fungie. The map even includes the Dublin Zoo and a Viking ship!

CUTE AND COZY DETAILS!

Shelling Out

Karla Courtney travels around dressed as a giant lobster! She designed and knitted the bright-red suit by hand. It took nearly 50,000 stitches to complete! It has giant claws and a tail hole so she can walk while wearing it! Based in the UK, Karla has worn the outfit on Brighton Beach, on the streets of Paris, and even on New York City's subway. She almost lost a claw while on the Staten Island Ferry! Karla says she loves lobsters and feels a special tie to them, as her grandfather was a retired lobster fisherman.

BOTTLE BALANCE

Bekah Burke walks along glass bottles while on her tiptoes—without falling off!

Bekah is a ballet dancer. She performs circus arts, too. One day she saw a photo from 1958 of ballerina Bianca Passarge walking on bottles. Bekah decided to give it a try! She practiced for hundreds of hours. Bekah has now mastered different "en-pointe" skills. She can walk from bottle to bottle without knocking over any. She can stand on one leg in a classic ballerina pose. And she can stand on two bottles, crouch down to pick something up, and stand again. Bekah makes it look so easy!

BEKAH'S INSPIRATION!

HIGH ENERGY ↗ Joel Spears from Rhode Island has built up a collection of more than 1,000 energy drink cans. He reviews energy drinks on his "CaffeineMan" YouTube channel.

HAND MAGNETS ↗ Body modification enthusiasts Sadie Riendeau and her fiancée Hannah Hansman have a real connection. The Massachusetts couple has small magnets implanted beneath the skin of their hands. So whenever their hands are near each other, their bodies physically connect.

SUPREME ATHLETE ↗ Native American athlete Jim Thorpe played baseball, football, and basketball professionally. He won Olympic gold medals in the decathlon and pentathlon. If that wasn't enough, he was also the 1912 intercollegiate ballroom dancing champion.

MEAN TRICK

After defeating Richard III at the Battle of Bosworth in 1485, King Henry VII of England had a sneaky idea. He officially backdated the start of his reign by one day. This meant that anyone who had fought against him at the battle could be charged with treason.

LIFE SAVER ↗ In his seven years as a young lifeguard in Illinois, future U.S. president Ronald Reagan was credited with saving the lives of 77 people.

BEDPAN COLLECTOR ↗ England's Mary Jacobs has been collecting bedpans since 1984. She now has more than 160 bedpans in all shapes and sizes. She purchased her first one at a garage sale for almost 70 cents, and her most expensive buy was about $24.

BROKEN LEG ↗ English athlete Rose Harvey ran an Olympic marathon with a broken leg. She suffered a stress fracture of her femur just 2 miles (3.2 km) into the 26.2-mile (42.2-km) marathon at the 2024 Paris Olympics. She finished in under three hours, even though she was in acute pain for almost the whole race.

Bag Ballet

Dancer Phia Ménard choreographed a ballet starring plastic bags that seem to dance through the air! The performance starts with her throwing colorful plastic bags into the air. Each bag is shaped like a human. And then the magic begins! The bags start to dance majestically before your eyes. But how? They move in a breeze created by fans cleverly placed around the stage.

Rock'n Reel

The "Fish-Caster" is a guitar like no other—it has a real piranha inside!

What started as a simple sketch became a musical masterpiece. Bobby Stirling and Greg Self of Stirling & Self, and Luis Orozco of Gepattos Guild, worked together on the *fin*-tastic project. At first, the fish was too thick, so they had to shave it down with a sander! Phew—it was stinky! They set the preserved piranha, an old lure, and a chunk of oak in blue-tinged resin. Then they secured the resin to the thin body of a Telecaster guitar. All in all, the project took four months. In the end, they made a guitar that not only rocks but also shows their love of fishing.

FISHING TRIP ↗ Peruvian fisherman Maximo Napa Castro spent 95 days adrift in the Pacific Ocean. His planned two-week trip changed when storms blew his boat off course. He survived by drinking rainwater and eating anything he could catch. This included sea birds, turtles, and even cockroaches. He was finally rescued by a fishing patrol boat nearly 700 miles (1,126.5 km) from land.

WRONG TUNE ↗ When Pedro Rodriguez won the 1967 South African Grand Prix, he was the first Mexican driver to win a Formula 1 event. Not expecting a Mexican victory, the live band didn't know how to play the Mexican national anthem. So they celebrated his win by playing the "Mexican Hat Dance" instead. After that, Rodriguez always carried a recording of the anthem with him to every Grand Prix.

FANTASTIC PHONE ↗ British YouTubers Arun Maini and Matthew Perks built an enormous iPhone that stands 6.74 feet (2.1 m) tall. They spent more than a year turning an 88-inch TV into a phone. The replica works just like a regular phone. It includes a touchscreen, camera, flashlight, and charging port. It weighs over 440 pounds (199.6 kg) and can send texts and emails. It cost more than $70,000 to make.

Back of the guitar

HE CAN TUNE A BANJO, BUT CAN HE TUNA FISH?

↗ FAN SHARE

Catchy Hook

Paul Hinton from South Carolina shared his fishing secret with Ripley's—playing the banjo! He discovered by accident that fish seem to like music. Paul wanted something to do while waiting for a bite, so he bought a banjo. But he didn't just play the instrument while his rod did the work. Instead, he attached a line and reel to the banjo! Now he's catching lots of fish, having fun, and entertaining those in and out of the water!

SHARE YOUR STORY AT
RIPLEYS.COM/SHARE

STILL GOT IT!

The Amazing Sladek has been thrilling audiences with his daredevil balancing act for almost 50 years!

Gary Borstelmann has loved gymnastics and acrobatics since he was kid living in Long Island, New York. At nearly 70 years old, he doesn't plan on stopping his death-defying stunts. His most famous act, the Tower of Chairs, involves no trickery or special equipment. He just needs nerves of steel and lots of practice! He stacks six chairs, one by one, until he's on top of a 25-foot-tall (7.6-m) tower. He then slowly moves into a perfect handstand—to rapturous applause!

Car Cemetery

In 2000, Michael Froehlich celebrated his 50th birthday in an unusual way: He bought 50 vintage cars that were all 50 years old! Instead of driving them, he parked the cars in a private forest near his home in western Germany. He was sure to remove the gas and other chemicals first. Now the forest grows around the cars as they rust and rot in this metal graveyard. Some of the cars could be worth millions if they were fixed up!

POPSICLE TOWER ↗ In São Paulo, Brazil, YouTubers Iberê Thenório and Mari Fulfaro created a 78.1-foot-high (23.8-m) tower of popsicle sticks.

SENIOR STUDENT ↗ In 2023, Minnie Payne earned a master's degree in interdisciplinary studies at the University of North Texas at age 90.

YOUNG INVENTOR ↗ Braille is the system of raised dots that helps visually impaired people read. It was invented in 1824 by France's Louis Braille when he was only 15 years old!

HANDSTAND CLIMBER ↗ Sun Guo Shan climbs Chinese mountains while balancing on his hands. In the handstand position he climbed his way up the 5,288.7-foot-high (1,612-m) Haibat Peak in the Wudang Mountains. He also climbed the 999 steps of Tianmen Mountain in five hours. That ascent was so challenging that he toppled over nearly 100 times.

EVERYONE WELCOME ↗ Every Sunday evening for more than 40 years, American Jim Haynes invited total strangers to his home in Paris, France, for dinner. Sometimes he entertained 120 guests at a time, which caused the dinner party to spill out into his backyard. Anyone wishing to attend just needed to contact him in advance. An estimated 150,000 people attended over the years.

Mini Marvel

Jean-Claude Fassler built his very own Eiffel Tower—right in his backyard! The retired metalworker from France spent eight years creating the replica. His grandson helped, too. Using tools from his workshop and the original 1889 plans, he brought his favorite landmark to life. The finished model is a 1/10 scale copy. It's a backyard masterpiece, made with skill, patience, and a big dream!

DAILY MARATHON ↗ During 2024, 55-year-old Belgian ultrarunner Hilde Dosogne ran a full marathon every day. Her 366 marathons covered around 9,596.5 miles (15,444 km).

PAPER DOLPHINS ↗ Iswarya Sundaralingam from England made 2,024 paper dolphins in eight weeks. She had been taught how to make them by a nurse while her mother was in the hospital.

DIZZY HEIGHTS ↗ Australian circus performer Charli Meath completed 53 aerial hoop somersaults in one minute at her gym in Victoria. It left her feeling so dizzy that she could barely stand afterward.

HANDLEBAR WHEELIE

Swedish stunt rider Magnus Carlsson hit a speed of 125.9 mph (202.6 kmph) on a motorcycle—while sitting on the handlebars and performing a wheelie! He also once traveled 190.1 miles (305.9 km) on a motorbike while sitting backward.

FREESTYLE FEAT ↗ In 2023, Ben Pobjoy from Toronto, Canada, ran 242 freestyle marathons—26.2-mile (42.2-km) runs over no set route—in nearly 70 different countries across North America, South America, Europe, Africa, and Asia.

STORE SLIPS ↗ Tyler Gyurisin of New Jersey spent three years collecting order slips from Wawa gas stations so that he could obtain a full set numbered 0–999. The quest required nearly 4,000 visits to Wawa, plus requests to friends to supply missing numbers.

PACKET TOWER ↗ In 2024, Lay's UAE (in the United Arab Emirates) built a 13.1-foot-tall (4-m) sculpture made entirely from hundreds of Lay's potato chip packets.

STEEP DROP DOWN!

SKY SKATER

Brazilian skateboarder Sandro Dias skated down a 22-story-high ramp!

Likely the tallest skate ramp in the world, it was built on the curved side of a government building in Porto Alegre, Brazil. A plywood ramp was built along the curve to make Sandro's ride safe and smooth. Sandro dropped from a height of 196.9 feet (60 m) and reached a whopping 64 mph (103 kmph), before hurtling into crash pillows to help him stop!

Supportive Sisters

The Bello Sisters perform breathtaking balancing acts—with just one person supporting the trio's weight!

Loren, Celine, and Joline have been practicing since they were kids. Acrobatics runs in the family! Their dad was in the Cirque du Soleil. Their mom was a high-wire performer. The Italian trio has put on shows for nearly 10 years. These acrobatic sisters amaze audiences when they become a human tower. With great strength, one sister supports the others as they balance on top of her—often upside down, too!

STRENGTH AND BALANCE!

Mane Mats

Farmers in Chile are using a new method to keep orchards alive during droughts—mats made of human and pet hair! The hair mats are placed around the bases of trees. They work by shading the soil and stopping water from escaping. The hair is sourced from 350 salons and 10 pet groomers. Each mat is woven by machine. The mats are compostable, which means they will eventually break down into soil.

FREE RIDES ↗ Canada's Courtney Allan hitchhiked all the way from England to South Africa. It took her almost a year. She caught 400 rides and traveled 8,000 miles (12,874.8 km) through 16 countries. And she only spent about $22 on transport costs over the entire trip.

MUSEUM DASH ↗ Ben Melham from Surrey, England, visited 42 London museums in a single day. He traveled between them on a kick scooter. There are more than 200 museums in the city of London. Ben's visits ranged from the Science Museum to the Cartoon Museum.

MOWER COLLECTION ↗ Englishmen Andrew Hall and Michael Duck have a collection of more than 1,500 lawn mowers. The oldest mower they own dates back to the 1830s. Their collection also includes the world's first motor mower and the third-oldest push mower.

DESTINED SINCE BIRTH!

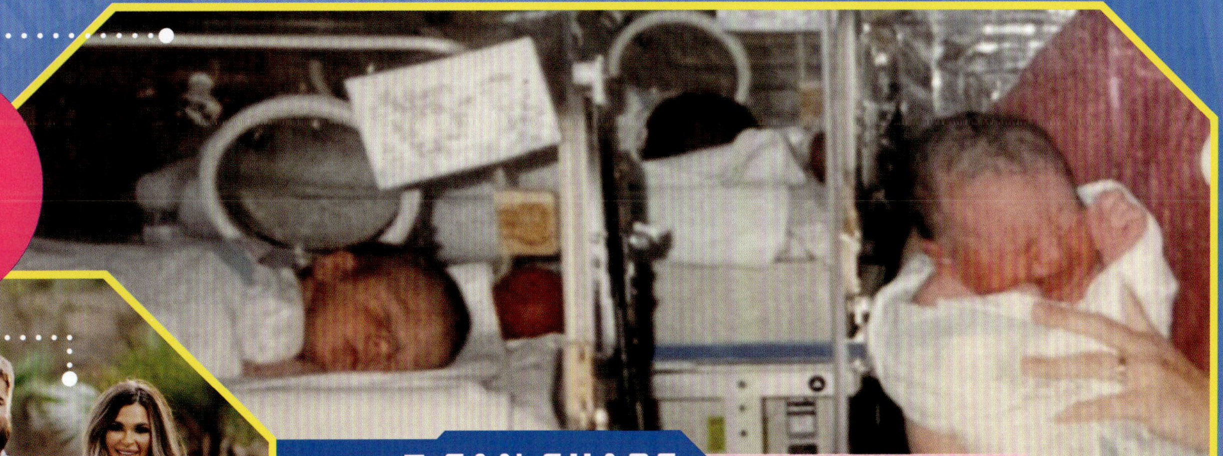

↗ FAN SHARE

Young Love

Imagine falling in love with someone and then finding out you first met 29 years ago—when you were born on the same day at the same hospital! This is the love story Shabree McQueen from Louisiana shared with Ripley's. Shabree and her husband were born just three hours apart but didn't meet until they were 29. They even have family photos showing their hospital cribs together! They married on their 31st birthday to celebrate their unique love story.

SHARE YOUR STORY AT
RIPLEYS.COM/SHARE

Reimagined REMAINS

Butch Anthony of Seale, Alabama, makes art out of bones—real ones!

In *The Persistence of Form in Life's Remains*, Butch shows off seven strange and amazing sculptures. One is a dress that he made from more than 500 pounds (226.8 kg) of animal bones! It is stitched together with electrical wire. Butch also created a piece called *The Bone House*. He had a dream about a house made from bones and decided to bring it to life. People can walk into the piece and sit on a bench that is placed inside.

OVER 500 POUNDS (226.8 KG) OF BONES!

The Bone House

Drive-Thru Museum

Butch Anthony doesn't just make bone art. In tiny Seale, Alabama, he created the Drive-Thru Museum! Packed with unusual art and curious sights, the galleries can be viewed without leaving your car! Butch built the museum in 2014 out of shipping containers. Some of his art can be seen inside, along with a mix of strange finds like a giant gallstone and a footprint that might be from Sasquatch! Anyone can visit the Drive-Thru Museum. It is open 24 hours a day, seven days a week.

Gallery interiors

DRIVE-THRU CURIOSITIES!

PHONY PREGNANCIES ↗ Italian Barbara Ioele was jailed for faking 17 pregnancies over a period of 24 years to receive around $100,000 in maternity benefits and claim time off work. She fooled colleagues by stuffing a pillow up her top, but the children she claimed to have birthed during that time never existed.

MOST WANTED ↗ Antonio "El Diablo" Riano was wanted for two decades in connection with a fatal shooting in Hamilton, Ohio, in 2004. He was finally located 20 years later in 2024. A determined detective tracked him down via Facebook and found that he was working as a police officer in Oaxaca, Mexico.

Dramatic Sneeze

While having breakfast with his wife, a 63-year-old Florida man sneezed so hard that stitches from a recent surgery split open. The man felt a sharp pain, and when he lifted his shirt, he saw several inches of intestine poking through the wound. He went on to make a full recovery.

MOON MISSION ↗ In 1970, about 24 hours into the Apollo 13 moon mission, astronaut Jack Swigert realized he had forgotten something major. He hadn't filed his tax return before the April 15 cutoff. The IRS agreed to extend his deadline on the grounds that he was a U.S. citizen abroad.

LOST CAMERA ↗ Shay Lalor lost his action camera in the ocean off the coast of British Columbia. Eight months later, it was found by scuba diver Ken Kieley about 30 feet (9.1 m) below the surface. Via social media he was able to trace Lalor and return the camera to him with its videos still intact.

COMPACT CAR

Andrea Marazzi, from Italy, built a working car that's only 20 inches (50.8 cm) wide!

Andrea used original parts from a 1993 Fiat Panda and reshaped them for his super-slim car. It has four wheels, a single seat, and a steering wheel. One of the few parts that didn't come from the original car is the electric motor. When fully charged, the car can travel up to 15 miles (24.1 km). It might take a while to travel that distance, though. The vehicle's top speed is just 9 mph (14.5 kmph)! Andrea isn't allowed to drive the car on normal roads, but he enjoys taking it to shows.

THAT'S A TIGHT SQUEEZE!

Hot Wheels

German engineer Marcel Paul upgraded a child's toy ride-on car to make it super fast! Marcel added a motor to the toy, hoping to exceed a speed of 88 mph (141.6 kmph). He worked on the project for 10 months. When it was time to test the toy car on a road, Marcel had to lie almost flat on his back to ride it. Amazingly, his modified, ride-on toy car reached a top speed of 92.2 mph (148.4 kmph)!

GOING OVER 90 MPH (144.8 KMPH)!

MOWING MAN ↗ To raise funds and support for men's mental health, Carlos Duque of Newcastle, Australia, pushed a lawn mower for 100.5 miles (161.7 km) in 24 hours in November 2024.

POTATO PLANT ↗ Cecelia Smith from North Carolina grew a potato plant that reached an amazing height of 11.25 feet (3.4 m).

MISSISSIPPI PADDLE ↗ At age 87, Dale Sanders paddled the length of the Mississippi River in 87 days. He paddled his 15.5-foot-long (4.7-m) canoe 2,350 miles (3,782 km) from Lake Itasca, Minnesota, to Luling, Louisiana.

PAST PINBALLS ↗ Rob Berk, the owner of Past Times Arcade in Ohio, has collected more than 1,000 different pinball machines, some dating back to the 1930s.

Zero to Kitty

This isn't your average car—it's a full-blown feline on wheels. Hayden and Helen Marks from Aylesbury, England, transformed their Audi A4 into the Meowdi. It's covered in yellow fur and has a pink nose with cute whiskers. It even has a tail and ears! Hayden and Helen decorated the vehicle for a car rally, where they raised money for the Cats Protection charity. The couple hopes to keep using the car to raise funds for good causes.

Hayden and Helen Marks

Heart in Hand

Jessica Manning from New Zealand keeps her old heart in a plastic bag!

Jessica was born with heart defects and has had 200 operations—including a heart transplant when she was 22 years old. She donated her heart to medical research. But 10 months later, she got a call asking if she'd like it back! The organ was vacuum sealed in a bag with formaldehyde fluid. It shouldn't start decomposing for 30 years—hopefully! When holding it in her hand, Jessica describes her heart as tough, like an old tire!

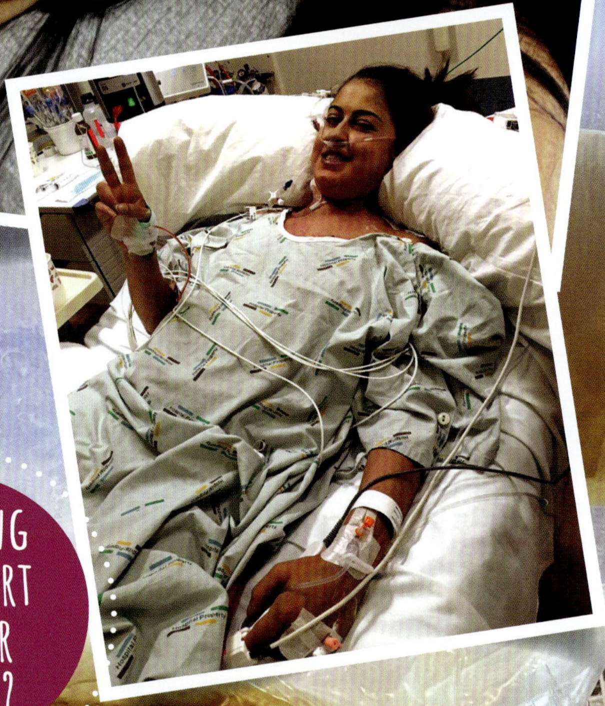

WEARING HER HEART ON HER SLEEVE?

Inked Forever

Artwork made from real skin is now a reality! Save My Ink Forever can take a loved one's tattoo after they pass and preserve it. The Ohio company is run by father-and-son team Kyle and Michael Sherwood. The two spent years perfecting their methods. They carefully remove and treat the tattooed skin, then frame it like art. The process takes about three months and gives families a way to remember loved ones.

REAL HUMAN SKIN!

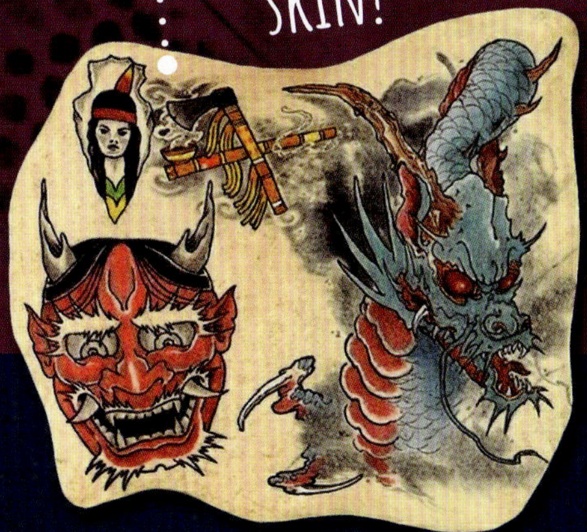

SCRABBLE CHAMP ↗ New Zealander Nigel Richards has won both the French and Spanish World Scrabble Championships. Amazingly, he can't speak either language!

LONG SPIN ↗ The Niagara Whirlpool has been spinning for 4,200 years. It is located downstream from Niagara Falls. When the Niagara River is at full flow, the 128-foot-deep (39.1-m) whirlpool spins in a counterclockwise direction. But when the river flow drops, the direction reverses.

MATH HOMEWORK ↗ A 10-year-old boy made an unusual 911 call—to ask for help with his math homework! The Shawano County Sheriff's Office in Wisconsin sent Deputy Chase Mason to the caller's home. He was soon able to solve the decimal-related math problem. But the sheriff also reminded kids that 911 calls are for real emergencies—not schoolwork.

↗ FAN SHARE

Pencil Power

Pennsylvania teacher Jason Stanko used the same mechanical pencil from first grade all the way through college! He told Ripley's that he estimates he used the pencil to write 25,000 pages of notes over 15 years. Jason didn't even include tests or homework in that tally! The green pencil has been repaired lots of times with new parts and tape. When he finished school, Jason chose to retire it. Now he displays it in his classroom along with his diploma to inspire his students!

SHARE YOUR STORY AT
RIPLEYS.COM/SHARE

LONG LIVE THE PENCIL!

DAUNTLESS DUO

LOOK! NO HANDS!

Anngela Burt can perform acrobatics at the top of a tall pole while it is balanced on her circus partner's face!

The pole can reach a nerve-wracking 30 feet (9.1 m) tall! Anngela and her partner, Jon Dutch, call themselves the Dauntless Duo. They travel around the United States, performing in circus and halftime shows. While Anngela balances upside down on her head at the top of the pole—sometimes with no hands—Jon often performs tricks of his own at the bottom! He can balance the pole and Anngela's weight while juggling. Talk about multitasking!

TEAMWORK MAKES THE DREAM WORK!

Hair Hats

Fashion brand Collina Strada made hats out of an unusual material—hair! Hairstylist Mustafa Yanaz is the creator who brought the hats to life. He said the concept started off as a joke, but he was all for the challenge. The hats were made from both fake hair and real human hair. He turned both classic baseball caps and beanies into unique works of art.

MAGICIANS TRICKED ↗ British magician Sophie Lloyd dressed up as a man in order to join a society of magicians known as the Magic Circle. She called herself Raymond Lloyd. Her disguise fooled the Circle for eight months. She finally revealed her true identity in 1991 when the rules were changed to allow women to join. However, the Circle did not like being tricked and promptly revoked her membership.

SHAKER COLLECTION ↗ Sharon Tidwell from Arkansas collected salt and pepper shakers for nearly 40 years. She picked them up at flea markets, from yard sales, and on her travels. She had Christmas shakers, Halloween shakers, and shakers modeled after pop culture icons. She had 1,150 shakers in total.

SINGLE BREATH ↗ Egyptian free diver Ramy Abdelhamid can perform 33 pull-ups underwater on a single breath. He did it at a depth of 29.5 feet (9 m) below the surface of the Red Sea.

SPEED CHOPPING ↗ Canadian chef Wallace Wong can use a knife to slice 125 celery chunks in 30 seconds. And he can do it while blindfolded. The former bodybuilder is known as the "Six Pack Chef."

ROLLER COASTERS ↗ Sean Evans is a professional roller coaster rider. Yet he is afraid of heights! He has been on about 130 different coasters around the world. He once rode Nemesis at Alton Towers near his home in England 64 times in six hours.

BLIND SHOT ↗ At a gym in Scottsdale, Arizona, Jeremy Ware sank an underhand basketball shot from 60 feet (18.3 m) away—while blindfolded!

RIPLEY'S COLLECTION

SEE MORE!

EXHIBIT NO. 16683

Hairy Handbag

Lyndall "Granny" Toothman made this purse out of her own hair! Granny spent much of her life teaching people the lost art of spinning and weaving. She could spin yarn out of almost any fiber. Dog fur was one of her favorites. But she also spun cat hair, camel fur, horse mane, and even baby penguin fuzz!

Afro Art

Hair artist Ava Marie shapes her hair into amazing sculptures!

Ava Marie is known as Kwiin Ava on social media, where she shares her unique creations. Ava squashes, twists, and pulls on her curls to form fun shapes. She has made all kinds of designs, from a cactus and a sushi roll to a snowman and a bird's nest. Some of the hair sculptures can take a while, especially when she needs to paint sections of her hair. But Ava can create some, such as a simple butterfly shape, in just minutes!

LEAPS of FAITH

Ivan Arestov from Sarasota, Florida, doesn't just ride unicycles—he jumps between them!

The circus artist pedals full speed on a unicycle that has no seat. Next, he leaps through the air, landing on a second moving unicycle. But that's not all! He then jumps to a third unicycle to finish the impressive trick. Ivan says it was a challenge to learn. He hit his shins a lot while mastering the stunt. Luckily, he now finds it super fun to do!

CUBAN BORN ↗ All three medalists in the 2024 Olympic men's triple jump were born in Cuba, but none of them represented Cuba in the Olympics! Gold medalist Jordan Alejandro Díaz Fortún represented Spain. Silver medalist Pedro Pichardo represented Portugal. And bronze medalist Andy Díaz Hernández represented Italy.

FIVE-DAY GAME ↗ A group of men played a continuous game of basketball for more than five days. They played for 121 hours 3 minutes at a school gym in Fairburn, Georgia. A total of 23 players took part, ranging in age from 17 to 64. The final score was 13,096 points to 12,972.

PLANE PULL

Italy's Matteo Pavone pulled three small airplanes while walking on his hands. Each plane weighed more than 5 tons, so he pulled a combined weight of over 15 tons.

PEDAL POWER ↗ Lael Wilcox from Alaska biked around the world in 108 days, 12 hours, and 12 minutes. Starting and finishing in Chicago, she rode a distance of 18,125 miles (29,169.4 km). She crossed 21 countries on four continents. She cycled up to 14 hours a day.

UNICYCLE RIDE ↗ Eamonn Keaveney rode a unicycle the entire length of Ireland. He pedaled 308 miles (495.7 km) from the southernmost point, Mizen Head, to the northernmost point, Malin Head. It took him 5 days, 5 hours, and 23 minutes. Previously, he had walked more than 1,200 miles (1,931.2 km) barefoot around Ireland.

↗ FAN SHARE

Ski Strings

The Macías family from Windermere, Florida, shared their amazing creation with Ripley's: working water skis made out of real guitars! Music and water skiing have always been a part of the family's life, so they merged the two. It wasn't always easy to get the musical skis to work. They ran into an issue when the guitars filled up with water! After some trial and error, the problem was fixed. The family says they already have a few new ideas for what type of wild skis they'd like to make next!

SHARE YOUR STORY AT
RIPLEYS.COM/SHARE

The Macías family also built these record-breaking skis that are nearly 20 feet (6.1 m) long!

CARDBOARD Creatures

London-based artist Josh Gluckstein makes life-size animal sculptures out of recycled cardboard!

He started to use cardboard in 2020 and has since made more than 80 cardboard creations! In 2024, Josh created a large 3D sculpture of a coral reef with over 50 different sea creatures. It is about 8 feet (2.4 m) tall and includes colorful fish, turtles, and eels. The piece took him four months to make! He has loved wildlife since he was a child and often works with charities that care for nature.

AMAZING WILDLIFE SCULPTURES

Special Sauce

The winning team of Duke University's Mayo Bowl football game in Charlotte, North Carolina, dumps 5 gallons (18.9 liters) of mayonnaise on their coach! It's a "reward" for leading them to victory! The saucy tradition started in 2021. More than 73,000 fans attend the event each year. It's taken very seriously, with practice mayo dumps and about 30 minutes of stirring to make the mayo perfectly runny. Yum?

TICKET QUEST ↗ Since 2020, Elliott Badger has been on a mission to collect train tickets. He wants to collect a ticket from each of the 2,700 stations with connections to Northampton, England. He displays the orange cardboard tickets in alphabetical order on a board at Northampton Station. By the end of 2024, he had collected more than 2,100.

RUNNING MATES ↗ Beginning on December 18, 2022, Aaron Robinson from London, England, ran 410 marathons in 410 days, accompanied by his two border collie dogs, River and Inca. He would get up at 3:00 a.m., run 26.2 miles (42.2 km), and then do a full day's work.

STICK REVIEWS ↗ In 2023, friends Boone Hogg and Logan Jugler found an interestingly shaped stick while on a trail in Utah. They filmed Jugler reviewing it and began posting similar videos online as a joke. It took off. Now millions of people follow the account, calling themselves "Stick Nation" and sharing reviews of unique sticks with each other.

FINAL PERFORMANCE ↗ Oscar-winning actor Marlon Brando's last performance before his death was recording dialogue for the 2006 video game *The Godfather.* Brando needed to wear an oxygen mask because of his poor health. This muffled his iconic voice, so a lot of his recordings were unusable for the final game. A soundalike actor was brought in to help finish his contribution.

RIPLEY'S COLLECTION

SEE MORE!

EXHIBIT NO. 166264

Water Colors

Alberto Cristini of Italy painted this scene while swimming in New York City's East River! Both an artist and a marathon swimmer, he built a floating easel so he could combine his two passions. With it, Alberto has painted shorelines of cities around the world!

BRUSHING UP

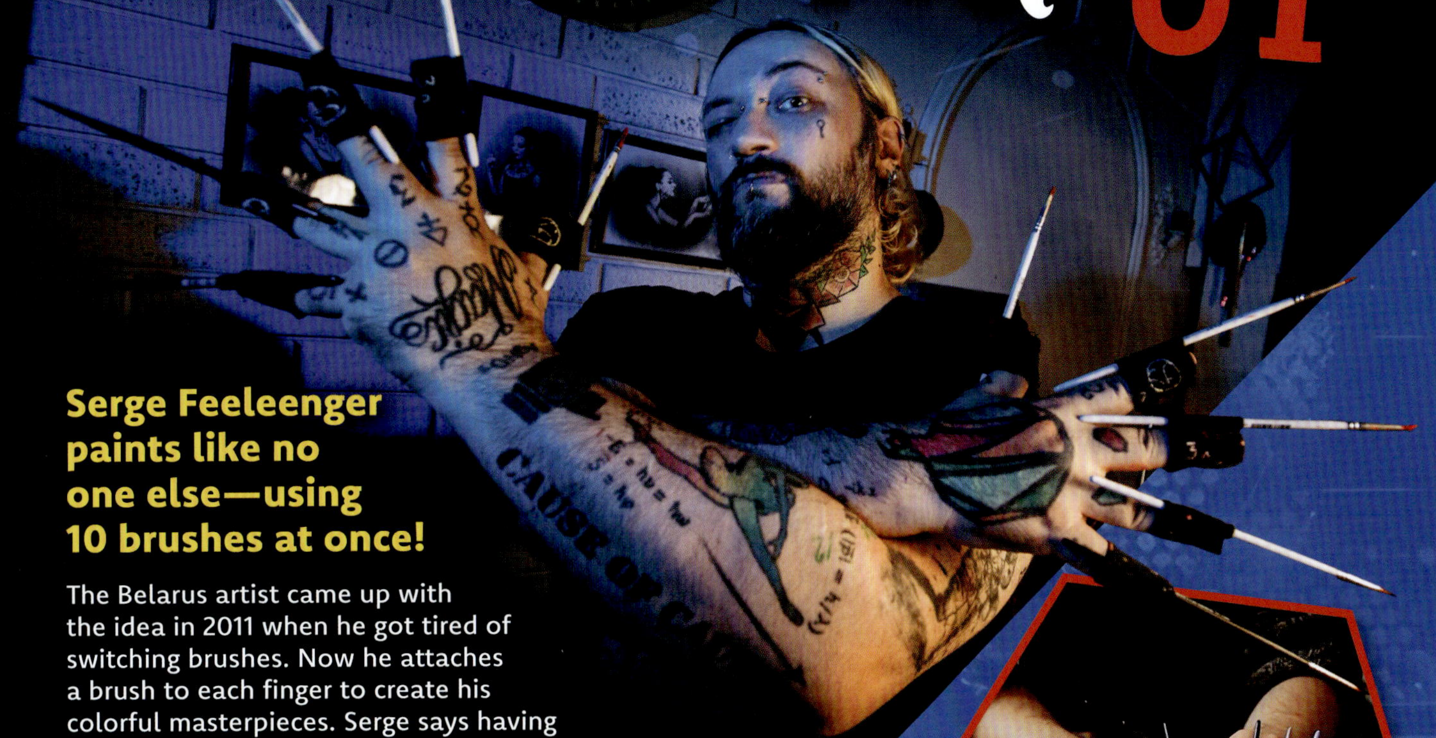

Serge Feeleenger paints like no one else—using 10 brushes at once!

The Belarus artist came up with the idea in 2011 when he got tired of switching brushes. Now he attaches a brush to each finger to create his colorful masterpieces. Serge says having 10 brushes on hand allows him to paint faster. He is self-taught and has practiced the technique with a variety of art styles. His one-of-a-kind approach wows his fans around the world.

ONE BRUSH ON EACH FINGER!

HIGH NOTE

Swiss musician Alain Roche took music to new heights—32 feet (9.8 m) above the ground, to be exact!

Alain played his piano while hanging from a crane. He performed every morning before sunrise for 182 days, starting on December 22, 2023, and ending on June 20, 2024. Alain changed the music a little each day, based on the sounds of nature he heard. He wanted to use his music to show how nature changes with the seasons.

JUVENILE JOURNEY ↗ Journey Castillo, from San Antonio, Texas, visited all 63 U.S. national parks by the time she had just turned three. When she was just a few days old, her parents, Eric and Valerie, drove her to Pikes Peak in Colorado, and that gave them the idea of taking her to every national park as quickly as possible. Their last stop was Lake Clark, Alaska, shortly after her third birthday.

CANDY CHAIN ↗ Elizabeth Allen of South Carolina spent four years folding 10,000 Starburst candy wrappers into a 195-foot-long (59.4-m) chain.

STILT STUNT ↗ While walking on stilts, 721 members of the Karbi community in Assam, India, formed a line that stretched for 1.24 miles (2 km). Stilt walking is part of Karbi culture.

TEEN STRONGMAN ↗ At 18 years old, Armenian Grigor Manukyan performed 44 pullups on a bar fixed between two moving trucks.

PADDLE PATH ↗ On October 2, 2023, Mark Walton of Ireland made the 23.6-mile (38-km) crossing of the English Channel in 3 hours, 54 minutes, and 50 seconds while lying down on a paddleboard.

↗ FAN SHARE

Sink or Swim

Kerry Haulotte of Riverside, Illinois, made a suit out of more than 1,150 bottle corks—and it floats! Kerry's stepdaughter Haley was so proud of her stepdad's cool creation that she told Ripley's all about it! To make the suit, Kerry drilled holes through corks and connected them like a string of pearls. He spent more than 130 hours stringing corks together in his spare time. When he finished, the suit weighed about 14 pounds (6.4 kg)! Kerry was nervous to test it. What if people thought his idea was silly? What if he sank? But he tried it anyway. It worked, and everyone loved it! Now everyone wants to try floating in the cork suit!

SHARE YOUR STORY AT
RIPLEYS.COM/SHARE

Indiana Stones

What's a good name for an adventurer who lifts really heavy rocks? Indiana Stones, of course! Meet David Keohan of Ireland. He came up with the name "Indiana Stones" when his local gym closed and he started stone lifting instead. David wants to bring back an old Irish tradition of lifting heavy stones. In Irish folklore, this was a way to show strength. On November 2, 2024, in Owning, Ireland, David lifted a big stone called "The Bulk," which weighed about 375 pounds (170.1 kg)!

DASH & Splash

At St. Peter's Fiesta in Gloucester, Massachusetts, brave contestants try to race across a grease-covered telephone pole without falling off!

The 45-foot-long (13.7-m) pole has one end on a platform in the harbor. It stretches out over the water, with a small flag waiting at the far end. The goal is simple: Stay on the pole long enough to grab the flag. But the thick grease makes that nearly impossible! Most people find themselves splashing into the water below. This slippery tradition began in 1931 and still thrills crowds today.

GRAB THE FLAG BEFORE YOU FALL!

COVERED IN SLIPPERY GREASE!

SUCCESS!

Canal Crossing

Thrill seekers in the Netherlands pole-vault over canals for fun! This long leap was once used by farmers to get across the waterways quickly. To take part in the sport, competitors take a big run up, push the pole into the water, and propel their body forward to—hopefully—land on the other side. The winner is the one who lands the furthest distance from the canal. The unlucky ones are . . . wet!

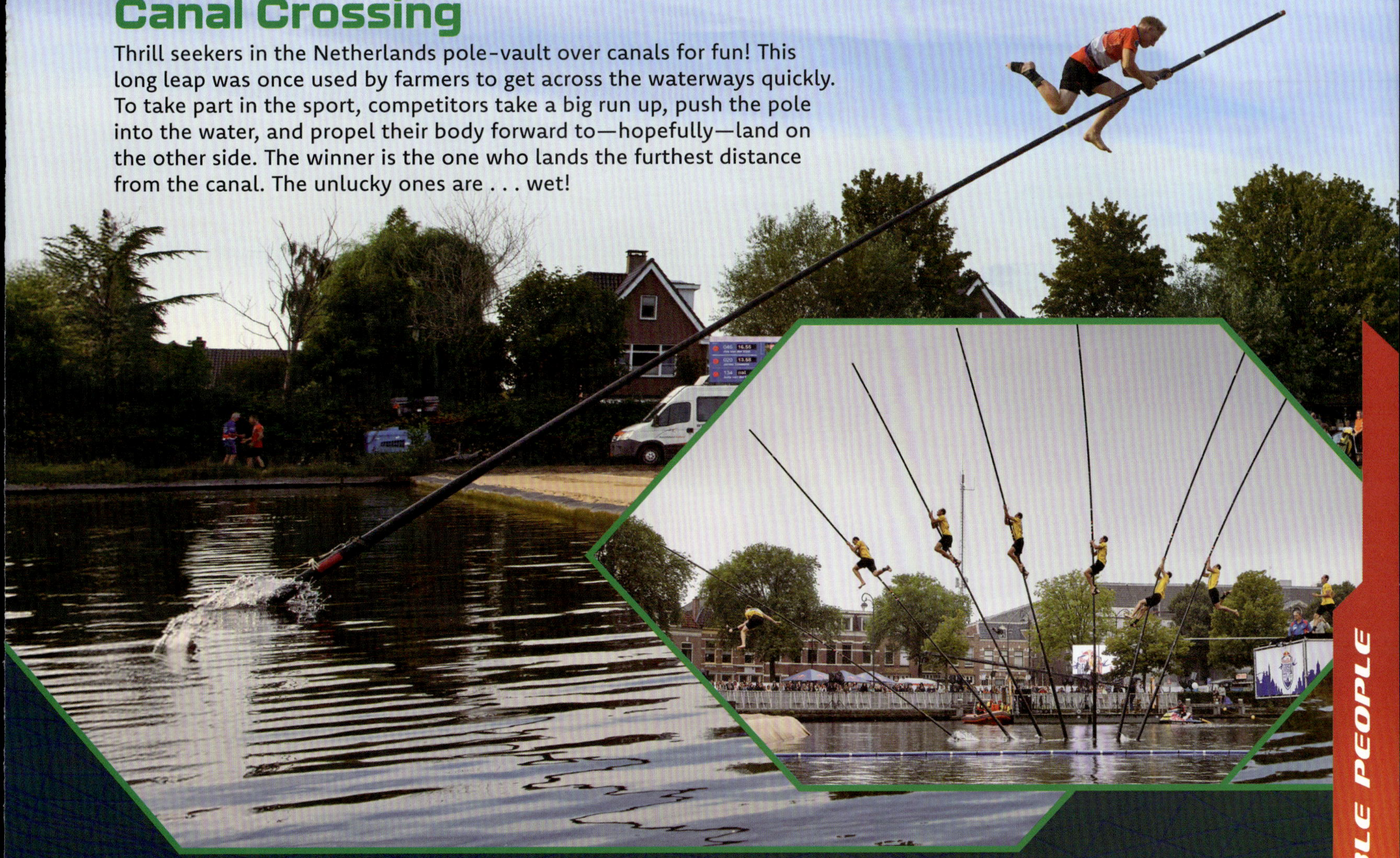

A Cut Above

In the Stihl Timbersports Championship, skilled lumberjacks go saw-to-saw to become world champion woodchoppers! For the springboard event, contestants must use their ax to chop through a block of wood at the top of a vertical log that is up to 9 feet (2.7 m) tall! The competitor first cuts a notch into the log at about shoulder height, then shoves a plank, or springboard, into the notch. They climb onto the plank, then repeat the process to get onto a second, higher plank. Now they must balance on the plank while they chop through the wood block on top. The best lumberjacks can do all this in less than 40 seconds!

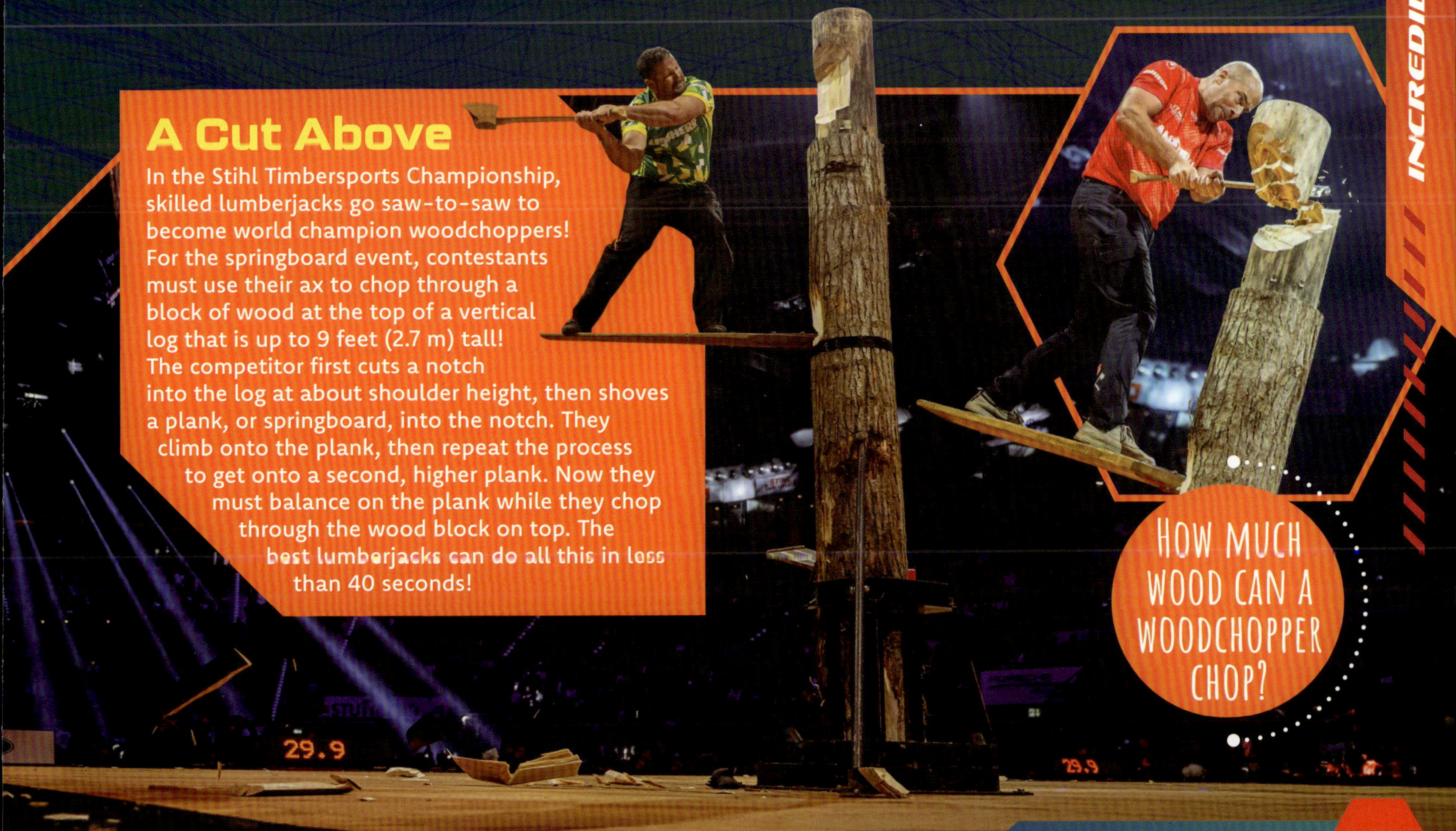

HOW MUCH WOOD CAN A WOODCHOPPER CHOP?

MIND-BLOWING BUBBLES

Italian bubble artist Luca Cutrupi performs in the dark—with glowing bubbles!

Performing under the name Sogni di Sapone, Luca amazes audiences with his spectacular show. He uses a special mix to make his bubbles fluorescent. They glow all different colors when viewed under black lights. But it's what he does with the bubbles that takes Luca's act to the next level. He can hold them in his hands, smoosh them together, and fill them with fog. He can blow bubbles within bubbles. He can even make giant bubbles that are bigger than himself!

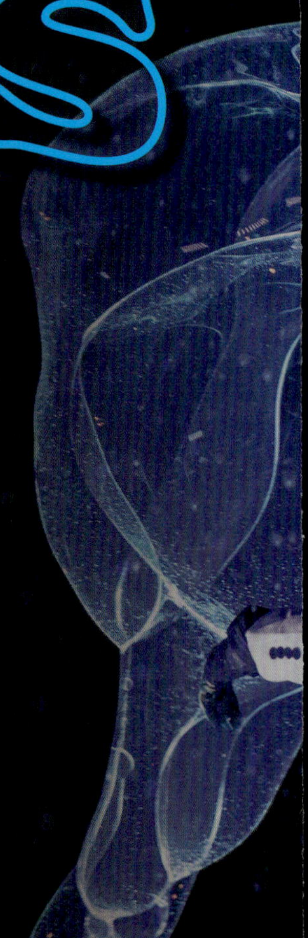

ARENA TOUR In November 2025, Ashvin Lad of Chicago, Illinois, became the 27th member of Club 124—people who have seen a game at every major baseball, basketball, football, and hockey arena in the U.S. and Canada. The feat was part of Lad's goal to live life to the fullest after beating cancer in 2000. The last stop on his list was UBS Arena in Elmont, New York. He picked a November 22, 2025, hockey match at the arena to mark the end of his tour—only to later learn that the game was an Islanders' "Hockey Fights Cancer" event.

BEYOND GOLD Filipino gymnast Carlos Yulo captured the hearts of his nation at the 2024 Paris Olympics. He won gold in both the floor exercise and vault events. His rewards included a fully furnished three-bedroom home, free phone cases for life, a lifetime supply of free buffets, and free tooth extractions.

FAST FEAST American competitive eater Raina Huang can eat 100 dumplings in 10 minutes.

EGG RACE At the 2024 Egg Fair in Mexico, more than 2,600 students from a local high school took part in an egg-and-spoon race. They each walked 330 feet (97.5 m) while trying to balance an egg on a spoon.

KIDNEY TRANSPLANT When singer and actress Selena Gomez received a kidney transplant in 2017, she decided to give her new kidney a name. She called it "Fred" after comedian Fred Armisen. He created and starred in her favorite TV show, *Portlandia*.

ICONIC AX The ax used by actor Jack Nicholson to chop through a door in the 1980 horror movie *The Shining* was sold at auction in 2019 for over $205,000.

KEEN COLLECTORS Father and son Lee and William Thompson from Bourbonnais, Illinois, are huge *Doctor Who* fans. They have collected more than 7,500 items of memorabilia relating to the sci-fi TV show—and they only started the collection in 2020!

CHEESE BALL

Two businesses in Mexico teamed up to make a string cheese ball that weighed 1,402.6 pounds (636.2 kg). It was made from over 2,641.7 gallons (10,000 liters) of milk. The cheese makers used a rotating table to create the giant ball.

Conker Conquest

At the World Conker Championships in Southwick, England, people bash each other's seeds on strings! Participants choose a strong and battle-worthy seed of the horse chestnut tree, called a "conker" in the UK. They make a hole in it and thread it on a string or shoelace. Each player has three tries to hit their opponent's conker with their own. They do this by swinging the conker down, like a hammer. If your conker breaks, you're out. Whoever conquers all the conkers is crowned the "Conker Champion!"

CIRCUS BLUES

Five Kenyan acrobats flipped their way from circus school to world stages as the Black Blues Brothers!

Their wild show mixes Kenyan acrobat skills with the rhythm-and-blues style of the 1980 film *The Blues Brothers*. The group says their act is a tribute to the famous fictional duo. Their high-energy shows amaze audiences around the world with music, jokes, and jaw-dropping tricks. During their act, there are flips, fire limbo, and human pyramids!

INGENIOUS ESCAPE ↗ Dr. Krisztina Ilko escaped from the bathroom of a medieval tower in 2024 using eyeliner and a cotton swab. She had been trapped in the tower at Cambridge University, England, for seven hours. Luckily, she remembered MacGyver—a fictional TV problem-solver she had watched as a child. So she picked the door lock by making a hook out of the cotton swab. She then used the eyeliner to push down the latch.

HIGH HAT ↗ Joshua Kiser, from Pennsylvania, built a hat that was a whopping 17.7 feet (5.4 m) tall. The hat was made from lightweight gutters and a trash can. These were reinforced with foam and covered in red fabric.

TOWER BLOCKS ↗ Miguel Angel Rodriguez has a tattoo of graffiti-covered skyscrapers on his back. The image of the abandoned Oceanwide Plaza in downtown Los Angeles was created by tattoo artist Eric Reyna. It covers nearly the entire length of Rodriguez's back.

Skateboard Challenge

Chad Caruso, of Long Island in New York, skateboarded coast to coast across the United States! He rode 3,162 miles (5,088.8 km) from Venice Beach, California, to Virginia Beach, Virginia, in 57 days, 6 hours, and 56 minutes. He averaged more than 55 miles (88.5 km) a day by skating for 10 hours.

IRON TONGUE ↗ Kranthi Kumar Panikera from India can stop electric fans with just his tongue. He can also insert a running power drill into his nose without spilling any blood. It has earned him the nickname of "DrillMan." His other stunts include hammering 22 nails into his nose in one minute. He has also pulled a vehicle weighing about 4,285 pounds (1,943.6 kg) by a sword held in his throat.

GIGANTIC JEANS ↗ Over 30 garment makers in China spent 18 days creating a ridiculously large pair of jeans. The pants measure 250.5 feet (76.4 m) long and have a waist circumference of 190.9 feet (58.2 m). It took 3.4 miles (5.5 km) of denim to craft the jeans. They weigh a hefty 7,936.6 pounds (3,600 kg). The zipper alone is more than 25 feet (7.6 m) long.

BRICK COLLECTOR ↗ Clem Reinkemeyer, of Oklahoma, has a collection of more than 8,800 different bricks. He has been collecting bricks for over 40 years. His oldest is a Roman brick that dates back more than 1,900 years to 100 AD.

FROM OUR 14TH ANNUAL BOOK!

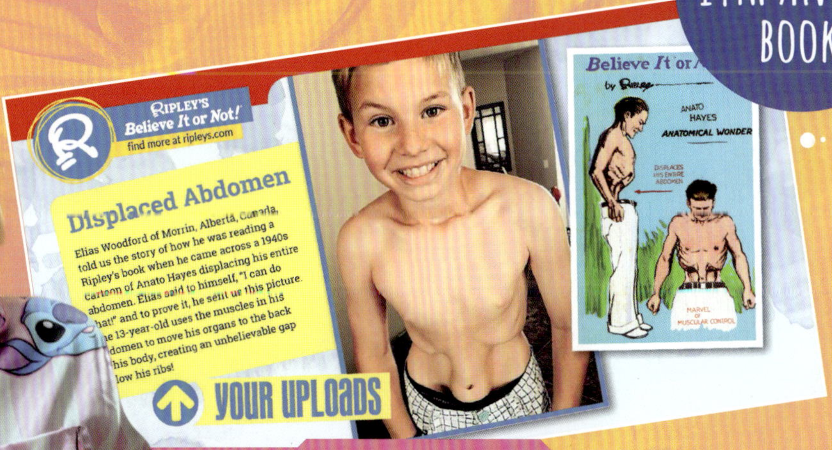

↗ FAN SHARE

Muscle Magic

Carys Jardine from Scotland got in touch with Ripley's to share a skill that she discovered while reading our book, *Ripley's Believe It or Not! Shatter Your Senses!* Carys was flicking through the pages when she saw a boy with a displaced abdomen. And eight-year-old Carys can do this, too! Carys concentrates hard, sucks in her stomach as far as she can, and holds her breath. It looks like her organs have disappeared, leaving huge gaps below her ribcage. Don't worry—although they move a little, the organs go back into place when she stops tensing those mighty muscles!

SHARE YOUR STORY AT
RIPLEYS.COM/SHARE

INCREDIBLE PEOPLE

APRIL 22 ↗ NATIONAL JELLY BEAN DAY

RIPLEY'S COLLECTION

EXHIBIT NO. 19011

Hidden Heist

In the 1870s, outlaw Jesse James stole a mailbag and hid it in the walls of a cabin near Kimberling City, Missouri. Nobody knew it was there for more than 70 years! It was found in the 1950s. The bag stayed hidden for decades, making it a mysterious treasure from one of America's most famous outlaws.

EXHIBIT NO. 176297

Card Chronicles

For 62 years, a simple Christmas card traveled back and forth between two friends. Bill Newton and Ronnie Ruoss exchanged the card every year. They added messages, doodles, and memories to the card. At one point the card was misplaced, and Bill had to track it down!

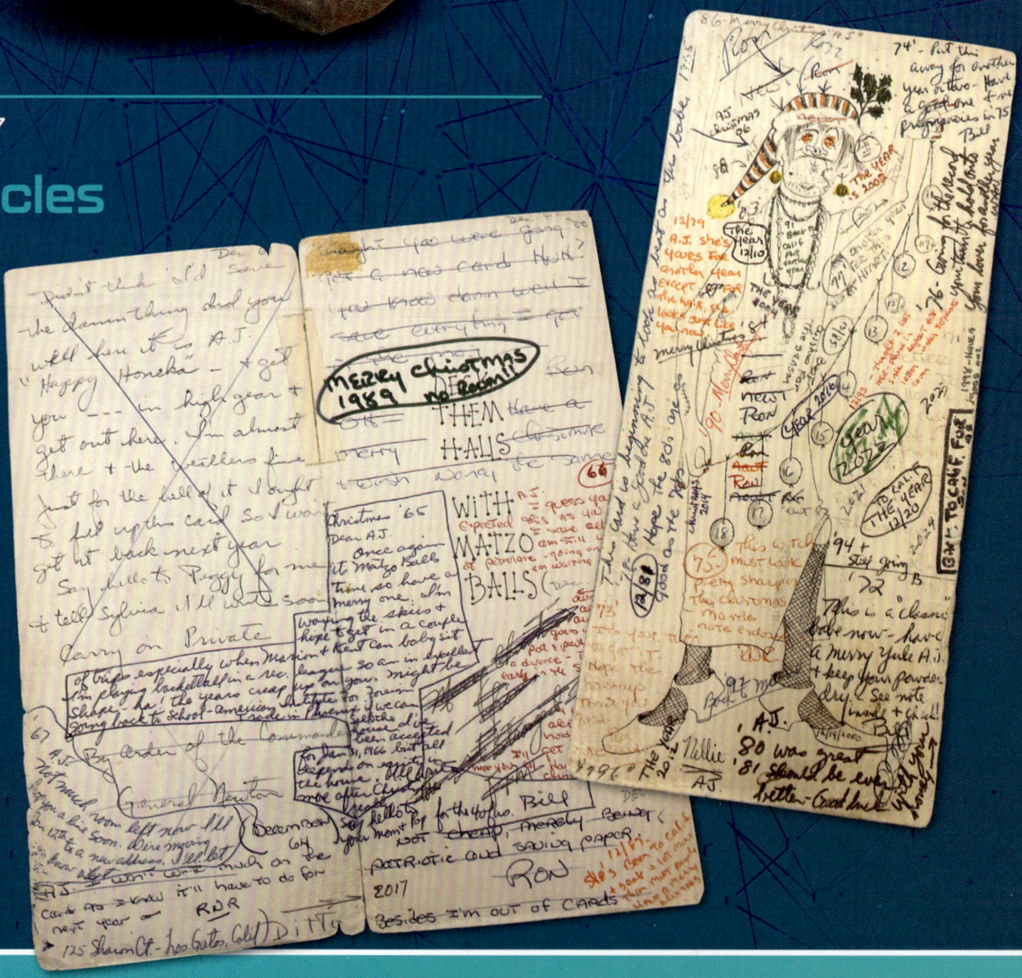

SEE MORE!

EXHIBIT NO. 172132

K'NEX Kingdom

This giant K'NEX ball machine, known as "The Citadel," is a moving maze of color and motion! It took Kyle Grubbs an entire year to build it. And it includes about 60,000 pieces! The machine has more than 45 fun parts, five different lifts, and tiny K'NEX people working like a busy factory. With catwalks, stairs, and balls racing everywhere, it's a wild build that never stops rolling.

UP NEXT...

NATURAL
WONDERS

SCORPION STROLLER

Imagine giving birth to up to 100 babies—and then carrying them around on your back for a few weeks! Believe it or not, that's the job of a scorpion mom.

Female scorpions give birth to live young, rather than eggs. The babies look like teeny scorpions, but they're much lighter in color and they can't sting. Their exoskeletons—outer bodies—are so soft, they'd stand no chance against a predator. Step in super-scorpion-mom! She lets them scramble up onto her back and pincers, ready to protect them with her life until their first molt, at about two weeks old. But there is a catch: If mom gets hungry, she picks off a few weaker babies and—gulp—has herself a snack! If they've survived this far, the babies leave mom to hunt and fend for themselves.

FEATHER LIGHT ↗ If you weighed 100 monarch butterflies together, the total weight would be less than 2 ounces (56.7 g).

MAIL MUNCH ↗ Snails were discovered living inside a mailbox in Devon, England. They ate the glue on the envelopes and left nibble marks on letters.

SWOLLEN SHARKS ↗ Swell sharks, which live in the eastern Pacific, swallow huge amounts of seawater so that their bodies swell to twice their normal size. This not only makes them appear more intimidating, it also enables them to wedge themselves into tight rocky crevices where predators cannot pull them out.

SWIM SAVE ↗ In October 2023, two small deer were rescued by state troopers off the coast of Alaska after being spotted swimming in the cold water an incredible 4 miles (6.4 km) from shore.

NO ESCAPE ↗ Snake teeth are curved backward to stop prey that is swallowed live and whole from escaping back out of the snake's mouth.

SHOE SLING ↗ When a child visiting Shendiao Mountain Wildlife Park in China accidentally dropped a shoe into the primate enclosure, a 14-year-old chimpanzee named Dong Dong tossed it back! At first the chimp played with the footwear, but when a keeper called for it to be returned to its owner, Dong Dong did as he was asked.

WATER WHIZZ ↗ Unlike most fish, the frogfish doesn't use its tail to swim. Instead it uses jet propulsion to move through the water, rhythmically gulping in water and then forcing it out through its backward-facing gills.

UN-*BILL*-IEVABLE BEAK

The sword-billed hummingbird from South America has a beak that's longer than its body!

The size gives the bird a big advantage while searching for food. It's able to get hard-to-reach nectar with little competition. However, its beak can sometimes be a challenge. The bird must use its feet to preen its feathers. Perching is also a balancing act! The bird has to carefully angle its bill so it doesn't lose its balance.

Desert Blooms

In 2024, flowers covered the Atacama Desert—in winter! Usually the white and purple blooms pop up in spring every few years. When they aren't blooming, the seeds wait underground. They start to grow when around 0.5 inches (1.3 cm) of rain falls and the temperature is just right. When heavy rains from El Niño arrived in 2024, the desert was awash with flowers for the first winter in nearly a decade!

FACT FILES

The Atacama Desert in Chile is said to be the oldest and driest desert in the world.

MIDGE MOB ↗ In April 2024, the village of Midgham in Berkshire, England, was plagued by swarms of thousands of midges! The tiny insects settled on cars, buildings, and people.

DANGEROUS DETERRENT ↗ To stop fans from running onto the pitch, the chairman of Romanian soccer club Steaua Nicolae Balcescu proposed building a moat around the playing field and filling it with crocodiles.

SUPER SWIMMERS ↗ Polar bears can swim vast distances in freezing waters with little rest. One female was recorded as swimming 426 miles (685.6 km) in nine days.

UNCOMMON CATCH ↗ A lobster caught off the coast of Maine in 2023 was not only half male and half female but also half blue and half orange—a one-in-50-million chance.

SOUTHERN CITIES ↗ Most Canadians live further south than the U.S. city of Seattle—in cities such as Montreal, Toronto, and Ottawa. About 90 percent of Canadians live within 100 miles (161 km) of the U.S. border.

MARINE GRIEF

Dolphins don't just leave their dead behind. Grieving mothers have been seen carrying dead calves on their backs for several days.

BRILLIANT BEARS ↗ Bears have occasionally been seen deliberately rolling rocks into bear traps to set them off and gain easy access to the bait.

CAT COMMUNICATION ↗ Cats have around 276 different facial expressions. Their range of expression is said to increase when they are domesticated and bond socially with each other.

CAMEL CONGESTION ↗ Camel riding in China's Kumtag Desert is so popular in the month of May that local authorities have installed several traffic lights in the sand dunes to avoid congestion. With up to 10,000 daily visitors and more than 2,000 camels available for hire, the lights are needed to stop camel riders so pedestrians can cross.

INNUMERABLE ISLANDS ↗ There are more than 50,000 islands in the Archipelago Sea, a stretch of the Baltic Sea near Finland. Most of them are uninhabited.

PERCHED *Pagoda*

Balancing on the edge of a cliff in Myanmar is a giant rock covered in gold!

This is Kyaiktiyo Pagoda. It is a sacred site for Buddhists. The rock itself is 25 feet (7.6 m) high and 50 feet (15.2 m) all the way around. A golden spire rises from the top. For thousands of years, pilgrims have covered the boulder in thin pieces of gold leaf—until it shines as brightly as it does today. Legend says that it doesn't roll off the cliff because it is held in place by a strand of Buddha's hair!

A GOLDEN TRADITION!

↗ FAN SHARE

Sticking Together

Lily Pittman shared this truly *tree*-mendous sight: two trees joined by three branches in Williamsburg, Virginia. This may have been caused by something called "inosculation." It happens when two branches rub against each other, which damages the bark. The trees repair the damage by growing new bark. The branches keep touching, and the new growth on both trees joins together. Over time, the branches simply become one!

SHARE YOUR STORY AT **RIPLEYS.COM/SHARE**

ZOMBIE SPIDERS ↗ A white fungus turns cave-dwelling spiders in Ireland into zombies. The parasitic fungus invades the spider's body and attacks its brain. It then forces the spider to crawl out of its cave and into the open, where it dies. This is a more suitable spot for the fungus to spread its spores and infect other unsuspecting creatures.

WALLET SNATCH ↗ A seagull snatched Noah Karberg's wallet outside of a grocery store in Nantucket, Massachusetts. The bird flew off with the wallet, which was stolen from a shopping cart. It then landed on the roof of a nearby car wash and picked through the wallet's contents.

LIFE SAVER ↗ Bear, a one-year-old golden retriever–husky mix, saved the life of his owner by keeping his heart beating. When Darren Cropper from Bonfield, Ontario, suffered a massive heart attack one night, Bear kept jumping on his chest for hours on end. He jumped so hard and for so long that his paw prints could be seen on Darren's skin. But Bear's actions kept Darren alive. Bear then ran upstairs to wake Darren's sleeping wife by leaping on her and howling in her ear.

Leafy Lodgings

These tiny bats work together to make a tent from a giant leaf! The Honduran white bats chew on the outer edge of a leaf to make it fold down—just like a tent. More than a dozen bats can snuggle together in one leafy home. In there, they hang upside down and find shelter from the sun. It also doubles as a great place to hide from predators!

NATURE'S *Perfume*

Some animals smell sweet, spicy, or just plain strange! The animal world is full of surprising scents. The smells often help creatures survive, attract mates, or mark their territory. Get ready to take a whiff of nature's perfume!

1 Binturong

The binturong, also called a bearcat, smells just like buttered popcorn! The scent comes from chemicals in its urine. They soak their feet and tail in it. This helps the binturong mark its territory and let others know where it's been.

2 Dogs

Ever notice your dog's paws smell like corn chips? That "Frito feet" smell comes from natural bacteria and yeast living on its skin. It's harmless and totally normal—just a funny reminder that even clean dogs can have their own scent.

3 Beavers

Beavers smell like a sweet treat! Vanilla, to be exact. The scent comes from castoreum. It's a liquid beavers produce to mark their territory. In the early twentieth century, the liquid was sometimes used in food or perfume.

Nutty
Signature
Scent

4 Spadefoot Toad

The spadefoot toad smells just like peanut butter! When scared, it releases the nutty scent from its skin. Scientists think the smell causes predators to stay away, as it can cause irritation if one gets too close.

Whoever
smelt it,
delta it!

5 Delta Smelt

The tiny delta smelt fish smells like fresh cucumbers! These fish are only found in California. If you hope to catch a whiff of these little swimmers, it could be difficult because they are currently critically endangered.

6 Kākāpō

This rare flightless parrot from New Zealand smells like sweet honey! Its soft, golden scent helps it stand out—but not always in a good way. The smell can attract predators, making this cuddly bird both charming and vulnerable.

WANT DAY **MAY 12** ↗ NATIONAL NUTTY FUDGE DAY

BUILDER BIRD

The male baya weaver crafts hanging nests that look like tiny woven baskets!

The baya weaver is a small bird found in parts of Asia. Using just his beak, the male weaves strips of grass and twigs into a cozy, curved structure. Each nest has a tunnel-like entrance to help keep predators out. The nest is built next to other weaver nests, often near water. A colony can have around 30 nests together! The baya weaver's nest is used to attract a female during mating season. If a female weaver approves, she will move into the home. If not, the male destroys it and starts over!

Diamond Beach

On a black sand beach in Iceland gleam giant glistening gems of . . . ice! The frozen fragments look so spectacular that the spot is called "Diamond Beach." The pieces of ice break away from a nearby glacier. They float out of a lagoon and then wash ashore on the beach. The "diamonds" eventually melt and disappear. Luckily, as the saying goes, diamonds are forever! And they're soon replaced by new sparkling jewels of the ocean.

Hardheaded

Take a hike in Joshua Tree National Park, California, and—yikes! Is that a giant skull? It certainly looks like one, but no. Over hundreds of years, rainfall has slowly eroded the granite rock. Two pockets of rock have worn away to make "eye sockets." Visitors to the park enjoy stopping by this creepy-looking stone. It's easy to see why it's called Skull Rock!

LEFT BEHIND BY A GIANT?

MONSTER BUG ↗ A new species of giant sea bug has been found off the coast of Vietnam. It is nearly 13 inches (33 cm) long and weighs 2.2 pounds (1 kg). This makes it as big as a guinea pig! The giant isopod has been named after Darth Vader because its body resembles his helmet in the *Star Wars* movies.

SOCK SNACK ↗ Luna, a young Bernese mountain dog, likes to chew things. But it got her into so much trouble that she needed lifesaving surgery in California after swallowing 44 items. These included 24 of her owner's socks, a shoe insert, a scrunchie, two hair ties, and a small onesie.

NEW SPECIES ↗ A new species of clearwing moth was discovered after hitching a ride inside photographer Ashleigh Cadet's bag. The stowaway moth larvae traveled 4,500 miles (7,242.1 km) from a jungle in Guyana to Wales. Three months later, two of them hatched on a windowsill of Ashleigh's home.

DAY **MAY 16** ↗ DRAWING DAY **MAY 17** ↗ NATIONAL

Tidal Trees

When the tide is low in China's Qiantang River, trees seem to appear on the riverbed! The pictures form when the water pushes channels through the soft sand and mud. The first push of water forms the "trunk." As the water's energy fades, it forms the "branches" and "twigs." If the temperatures are very cold, the water freezes in the tree shape! It looks amazing but doesn't last long, as it's quickly melted by the sun.

CLAW MACHINE ↗ A live groundhog was rescued from a claw machine. The creature was found hiding among the toys inside a claw machine at a mini-golf course in Duncansville, Pennsylvania.

UNWELCOME INTRUDER ↗ The eel-like pearlfish spends most of its life inside a sea cucumber. It enters the cucumber's body cavity through its butt. Then it uses the cucumber as a mobile home. It also feeds on the cucumber's insides.

CAMEL TRADE ↗ There are more than twice as many camels as koalas in Australia. More than one million camels live in the Australian deserts. There are so many that Saudi Arabia even imports camels from Australia.

SEVERED LEG ↗ Surfer Kai McKenzie was attacked by a 10-foot-long (3-m) great white shark near Port Macquarie, Australia. A few hours later, his severed right leg washed up on the beach. An off-duty police officer used a dog leash to stop the bleeding. Then Kai and his leg were flown to a hospital in Newcastle 124 miles (199.6 km) away. Although surgeons were unable to reattach his leg, Kai survived and returned to surfing after his recovery.

PLAYING DEAD ↗ When attacked, dice snakes often thrash around wildly and smear their body in their own poop. This stops animals or large birds from wanting to eat them. If that fails, they may play dead by falling limp with their mouth open and their tongue hanging out. Sometimes they even fill their mouth with bubbling blood.

ROCK POCKET ↗ Sea otters have a loose fold of fur under their armpits. This acts as a pocket where they store small rocks for cracking open shellfish. Some otters use the same rock over and over again.

Clear Caterpillar

The insides of a Brazilian skipper moth are on full view when it's still a caterpillar! Its head appears normal and the circulatory system is bright white. But its body is clear! If you look closely, its body looks a little green. This is because you can see the leaves it has eaten! The insects can be found year-round in parts of Florida, Texas, and Mexico.

Froggy Fingers

FACT FILES

Polydactyly is a condition where a person or animal is born with extra toes or fingers.

Soy is not your average Amazon milk frog—he has an extra hand!

It's fully functional and makes it look like he is waving. So cute! Soy was rescued by Jules White in 2024, and she has cared for him ever since. The tiny frog has gained a following on social media, as Jules shows him living his best life in sunny California. Jules thinks that one day this mini hand might just fall off!

Tree Tunnel

Who would've thought that a drive-thru would become a tourist attraction? A giant redwood in Klamath, California, has a tunnel cut through its 17-foot-diameter (5.4-m) trunk. Cars can travel straight through it! The roughly 800-year-old tree stands at 90 feet (27.4 m) tall. It was hollowed out in the 1970s so the tree didn't have to be removed in place of a road. Tens of thousands of people arrive every year to travel through the tree tunnel!

WEDDING PHOTOS ↗ Barry and Margaret Sharman from Penticton, British Columbia, finally got to see their wedding photos 56 years after they were married. They were married in 1968 but could not afford to buy the photos at the time. Years later, the wedding party photos were purchased at a garage sale. They eventually found their way to a local museum. Sandy Farynuk, who had been one of the couple's bridesmaids, worked there as the museum's president. After recognizing herself in the old black-and-white photos, she gave them to the Sharmans in December 2024.

AMPUTATED FINGER ↗ Australian field hockey player Matt Dawson decided to have part of his finger amputated so that he could compete at the 2024 Paris Olympics. He broke his finger in training two weeks before the Games. It would have taken months to recover from surgery to fix the break. So instead he chose to have the finger removed from the knuckle up. That meant he was fit enough to represent his country in France.

WOULD YOU DANCE IN A TREE?

Wooden Waltz

German villages used to have epic parties—in trees! These high-up dance halls were called "Tanzlinden," or dance lindens, after the kind of tree they were built inside. Linden trees have large branches that spread wide—the perfect place to build a dance floor! The village of Peesten in southeast Germany still has a dance linden. The roof and walls are shaped out of the tree's branches and leaves. Festivals, weddings, and music events are enjoyed there every year.

SUPER STUMP

A giant sequoia tree was chopped down in 1891, just to prove to the world that it was real!

People simply didn't believe that such huge trees existed. The 300-foot-tall (91.4-m) tree stood in what is now known as Kings Canyon National Park in California. It was named after author Mark Twain. The mighty task of cutting through the 16-foot-wide (4.9-m) trunk took about two weeks! One piece of the trunk was sent to a museum in New York. Another piece went to a museum in London. Then people could see the sequoia's size for themselves. The remaining stump is a top photo spot for tourists—still *stumped* by its size!

IT'S STILL HERE TO SEE TODAY!

NATURAL WONDERS

Neat Feet

The American coot's feet are perfectly adapted for life both in water and on land! Each toe has two or three large segments. The coot uses these wide lobes to push effortlessly through the water as it swims. But on land, it's a different story. As the coot lifts its leg to walk, the lobes get out of the way and fold back! So walking on mud, grass, or even snow is a cinch. But their party trick is running across the water's surface, before taking off into the sky. Wow!

EYES CLOSED ↗ Frogs use their eyeballs to help swallow food whole. Their eyeballs can be pulled back through holes in their skull. By closing their eyes while eating they are able to push downward with their eyelids. This forces the food in their mouths down their throat.

SMART DOG ↗ Athena, a four-year-old German Shepherd mix, went missing for nine days. She returned to her home in Green Cove Springs, Florida, at 2:30 a.m. on Christmas Eve by ringing the doorbell! Her family's Ring camera showed the smart dog pawing at the front door and jumping up as if to announce that she was home for the holidays!

GIFT WRAPPED ↗ When he wants to mate, the male nursery web spider brings the female a gift. What's more, he lovingly wraps it in silk. It is usually something to eat, such as insect larvae. If she approves, he mates with her while she unwraps and eats the meal. If the male can't find food, he may bring her a gift-wrapped twig instead and hope that she likes it.

GOAT RUNNER ↗ Heidi Taylor's 10-year-old goat Joshua escaped from his Newfoundland pumpkin patch and joined a half-marathon. He trotted alongside the 250 human athletes as they passed his home. Joshua completed the last 2.5 miles (4 km) of the 13.1-mile (21.1-km) race. The organizers were so impressed, they presented him with a medal!

HALF EGG ↗ Female erect-crested penguins always lay one-and-a-half eggs. The eggs are laid about five days apart. But the first egg is only around half the size of the second. The smaller egg is not incubated by the parents and never hatches. The birds know they can't feed two chicks. So they abandon one egg to ensure that the second survives.

MOUSE MEAL ↗ A Scandinavian Airlines flight from Norway to Spain was diverted to the Danish capital, Copenhagen. The emergency was caused by a live mouse crawling out of a passenger's in-flight meal!

Puppy Mountain

In Yichang, China, a mountain has locals and tourists doing double takes—it looks just like a giant dog's head! A hiker snapped a photo, and soon the rocky cliff was known as Puppy Mountain. Since then, crowds have come to see it for themselves. Some dog owners even bring their pets to pose beside the stone pup!

No Limb-its!

Autumn may have been born with only three legs, but her *paws-thetic* collection gives her loads of limbs to choose from!

Autumn's owner Diane Biegler shows off the looks that make her pooch a social media star. Autumn once dressed up as a pirate, with a peg leg and a box of treasures. While hanging out with her duck toy, she sported her own duck flipper! Believe it or not, to get ready for the beach, she sometimes straps on a shark fin or an octopus tentacle. That's not something you see every day!

FROM EVERYDAY TO DUCKDAY!

NATURAL WONDERS

WINGIN' IT

Most birdsongs are made with chirps and whistles, but the club-winged manakin makes music with its wings!

To do this, the male bird's body is pretty special. It has a club-shaped feather on each wing, solid wing bones, and large wing muscles. It raises its wings across its back and hits them together more than 100 times each second! The sound it makes is similar to a violin. Males use this unique "song" to attract females during courtship.

DOES SHE SEEM IMPRESSED?

FACT FILES

Making sound by rubbing body parts together is called "stridulation." It is common for insects, such as crickets, but extremely rare for vertebrates.

WILY WEASEL A weasel stole 22 slip-on shoes from a kindergarten in Japan. The children's shoes were stored in cubbyholes near the front door. The shoes went missing over a period of several days. But then the four-legged thief was finally caught on camera.

SHARK CAFÉ Large numbers of great white sharks regularly meet in a small area of the Pacific Ocean. The remote region is located midway between Baja California, Mexico, and Hawai'i. It is so popular with the fearsome predators that scientists have called it the White Shark Café.

MONKEY DETERRENT Some farmers in India dress up as bears to protect their crops from monkeys. Farmers in the village of Dhaurahra saved up to buy a bear costume. They take turns wearing it while patrolling their land.

RARE SIGHTING The New Holland mouse, a small Australian rodent, was first sighted in 1843. But it was not seen again for more than a century until its rediscovery in 1967.

PYRAMID CLIMB A paraglider was amazed to see a stray dog barking from atop the Great Pyramid of Giza in Egypt. How did the dog get to the top of the more than 450-foot-tall (137.2-m) pyramid? Nobody knows.

YODELING DOG The New Guinea singing dog doesn't bark like other dogs. Instead the animal, which is closely related to the Australian dingo, makes a strange yodeling sound. It sounds like the dog is singing.

LIVE FISH

Restaurants in Fukuoka, Japan, serve live fish. The dish is called *shirouo no odorigui*. Shirouo, or ice gobies, are small fish that are served in a shot glass and swallowed with a dash of soy sauce. The wriggling fish are said to dance down your throat!

The Wormhole

Right next to the ocean in Galway, Ireland, nature has carved out a perfectly rectangular pool! Known as the Wormhole, it sits near the bottom of some cliffs. Some of the water comes from underground; the rest comes from waves as they crash over the sides. You're not allowed to swim in it, though. The sides are high and it's easy to become trapped, but sometimes world diving competitions are held here! Expert divers have plunged a whopping 92 feet (28 m) into the water below!

RIPLEY'S COLLECTION

EXHIBIT NO. 15985

Stuck Skull

In 1930, naturalist Eugenia Shorrock stumbled across this odd find in the American West. About 100 years before she found it, a bighorn sheep rammed the tree and got stuck. The sheep never got free, and the tree grew around its skull and horns.

SEE MORE!

Droopy Dog

Caramel the dog has stretchy skin that makes him look like he's melting!

Caramel didn't always have saggy skin. He was found in 2020, weakly wandering the streets of central Florida with injured paws. These days, he's a happy pup living with his owners, Vladimir Lenk and Stephanie Cox, and their other pets. A few years after his rescue, Caramel's skin started to stretch. His vet had never seen anything like it! They think it is caused by Ehlers-Danlos syndrome. Luckily it doesn't stop Caramel from living a normal doggy life. He plays in the yard, chases cats, and yaps for treats, just like any other pooch!

Fact Files

Ehlers-Danlos syndrome affects the body's connective tissues. Humans, dogs, and other animals can be born with it. It can cause symptoms like stretchy skin and overly flexible joints.

FISHY MYSTERY ↗ Orcas sometimes wear dead salmon as hats. They have been seen swimming with the fishy headgear in the Northwest Pacific. But so far nobody knows why they do it.

COUNTING PLANTS ↗ Carnivorous Venus flytrap plants are able to count to five. They only close their jaws when two of the hairs on their leaves touch each other in a short span of time. And they only start digestion if five hairs are triggered. This ensures that they only use their energy on edible prey such as insects. They don't want to waste energy eating falling raindrops.

FLEXIBLE FEET ↗ The kinkajou is a small nocturnal mammal from Central and South America. It has a neat trick. It can rotate its hind feet 180 degrees—so they face in the opposite direction. This allows it to run and climb backward just as easily as forward.

SKATER DOG ↗ Chowder the bulldog loves to go skateboarding. He has been skateboarding for more than seven years—ever since he "borrowed" a boy's skimboard at an Oregon beach. His owners, Jami and Rich Delperdang from Fox Island, Washington State, could see that he loved it. So they ordered an extra-wide board to be made for him at a shop. Now he has 20 boards, including four electric ones. His impressive skills have earned him more than 1.5 million followers on TikTok. But he can be temperamental. If he has a bad run, he'll angrily flip the board over and growl at it!

Seabird 'Stache

The Inca tern looks like it has a handlebar mustache! It's actually a set of fine white feathers. It looks very striking next to its black plumage and red beak. And here's the wild part: Scientists say the longer the mustache, the healthier the bird. The Inca tern is found on the coasts of Peru and Chile. Both males and females grow these "staches!"

38 DOGS ↗ Mitchell Rudy from Alberta, Canada, took 38 dogs for a walk at the same time. He took the dogs on multiple leashes for a walk of 0.6 miles (1 km).

HIGH JUMP ↗ Nine-banded armadillos can jump 4 feet (1.2 m) in the air when startled. That is almost twice their body length. It would be the same as an adult man clearing 11 feet (3.4 m) in a high jump! This tactic allows armadillos to shock and confuse predators, giving them the chance to escape.

CLOSEST STATE ↗ Which U.S. state do you think is the closest to Africa? Believe it or not, it's Maine—and the distance is about 3,154 miles (5,075.8 km).

HAMSTER ESCAPE ↗ A Portuguese airplane was grounded after 132 hamsters escaped from the cargo hold. Workers at Ponta Delgada Airport in the Azores spent four days searching for the elusive rodents. They were worried that the hamsters could chew through the plane's electrical wires.

Long Lips

The slingjaw wrasse is a fish with a superfast extendable mouth! To catch its prey, its lower jaw drops down and then shoots out. It looks a bit like a wide straw and measures about half as long as its body. The deadly move takes just a fraction of a second! Small fish hiding among its coral reef home in the Indo-Pacific stand little chance. The slingjaw wrasse can also flip over stones and gulp down whatever is underneath. After swallowing tasty treats, it simply spits out anything unwanted.

PAWS WITH EXTRA TOES!

↗ FAN SHARE

Lasting Impressions

Mark Manning of the UK shared with us his unique collection—bricks with cat prints! He found his first one over 40 years ago, and the bricks have piled up ever since. Mark is a recently retired construction worker and found the unique bricks on job sites. He told Ripley's he is currently restoring a home. Believe it or not, he found even more immortalized paw prints in the process! Mark plans to place a few as accent pieces as he finishes his home.

SHARE YOUR STORY AT **RIPLEYS.COM/SHARE**

Mark Manning

Paw prints over 300 years old!

BIG FOOT ↗ A giraffe's feet measure about 12 inches (30.5 cm) across—the size of a dinner plate.

MEERKAT MERGER ↗ If a group of meerkats feels threatened, they stand together, arch their backs, raise their hair, and hiss to fool an attacker into thinking they are one large, vicious animal.

DOG DISASTER ↗ A fire at a house in Colorado Springs was started by a family's dog. Home security footage showed the dog jumping up and turning on a stove with its paws, igniting some boxes that were sitting on top. Although the burning kitchen set off a smoke alarm, which woke the family, the fire caused enough damage to force them and their dog to move out temporarily.

SILENT SESSIONS ↗ Kemptown Bookshop in Brighton, England, opens at 5:00 a.m. on the first Wednesday of every month so local writers can work in peace and quiet.

TOY TRIP

Friends Lauren Lee and Cassie Aran drove 596 miles (959.2 km) down the east coast of Florida from Jacksonville to Key West in toy convertible cars. The cars run on rechargeable batteries and have a maximum speed of 11 mph (17.7 kmph). The journey took them 58 days.

POOL DUEL ↗ At the inaugural Florida Man Games, held in St. Augustine in February 2024, competitors took part in a series of bizarre events, including dueling in an inflatable pool with weapons made from pool noodles and an "Evading Arrest Obstacle Course," where runners jumped fences to escape from real sheriff's deputies.

EARLY POWER ↗ In 1900, although both steam-powered and gasoline-powered vehicles were in production, 38 percent of American cars were electric.

LONE VOTER ↗ The region of Banej, India, has only one voter—Mahant Haridas Udaseen, a priest who lives deep within the Gir Forest. For a 2024 election, 10 officials traveled for two days by bus along unpaved roads to set up a special polling booth just so he could vote.

NIGHT VISION ↗ By law, pedestrians in Estonia must wear reflectors at night so they are visible in vehicle headlights.

COOL COCOON

Some caterpillars spin cocoons that look like tiny, gold baskets!

These wiggly weavers are part of a family of insects known as false burnet moths. They usually live in areas where it rains a lot. Scientists think the basket shape allows rain to pass through the cocoon so the pupa doesn't drown. But wouldn't having an open cocoon make the pupa an easy snack for predators? Not so! The caterpillar weaves its little basket at the end of a long silk thread. When birds peck at the cocoon, it simply sways away!

FACT FILES

A moth caterpillar makes a cocoon, but a butterfly caterpillar makes a chrysalis.

Forever Flakes

Danielle Oliver of Colorado turns fast-melting snowflakes into one-of-a-kind jewelry!

Preserving snowflakes is no easy task. To collect them, Danielle braves the freezing cold for hours at a time. She carefully places each snowflake onto a slide using a small paintbrush. Then she quickly coats them in a special resin. After weeks of curing, the flakes are ready for Danielle to add her final touches. It's hard work, and the smallest wrong move could destroy the snowflake. Ripley's caught up with Danielle to learn more about her art.

Q: What first inspired you to capture and preserve snowflakes?

A: It all started with my daughter and her first snowfall. Watching her experience snow for the first time, seeing her eyes light up with wonder, I thought, "I want to save this forever." I wanted her to hold onto a tiny piece of magic she could carry with her always.

Q: How did it feel when you preserved your first snowflake?

A: I felt pride and a dizzying sense of wonder. I knew immediately I wanted to share these moments, to give others a chance to see beauty they might otherwise miss.

Q: Are there patterns or shapes that surprise you?

A: Absolutely. Even after years of preserving snowflakes, I am continually amazed by nature's creativity. Some snowflakes display geometric precision, while others are wildly unique and intricate.

Q: How do you choose which snowflakes to keep?

A: I am drawn to snowflakes that stop me in my tracks, with shapes that seem almost impossible. Sometimes it feels like the snowflake chooses me as much as I choose it.

> Sometimes it feels like the snowflake chooses me as much as I choose it.

Danielle catches snowflakes with her daughter.

STEP 1
Catch snowflakes.

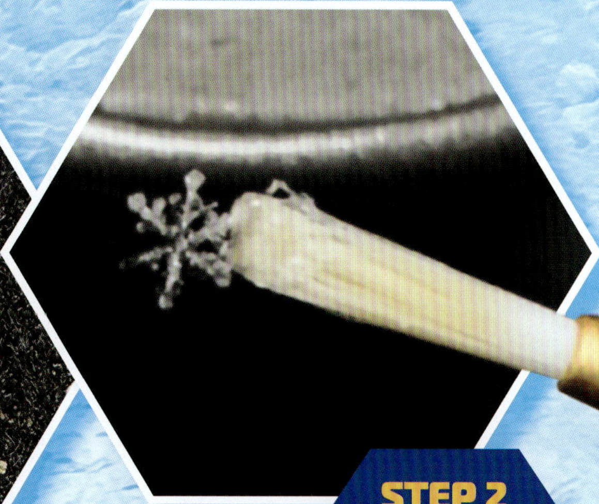

STEP 2
Place on slide and cure in resin.

STEP 3
Turn into wearable art!

GLIDE RIDE

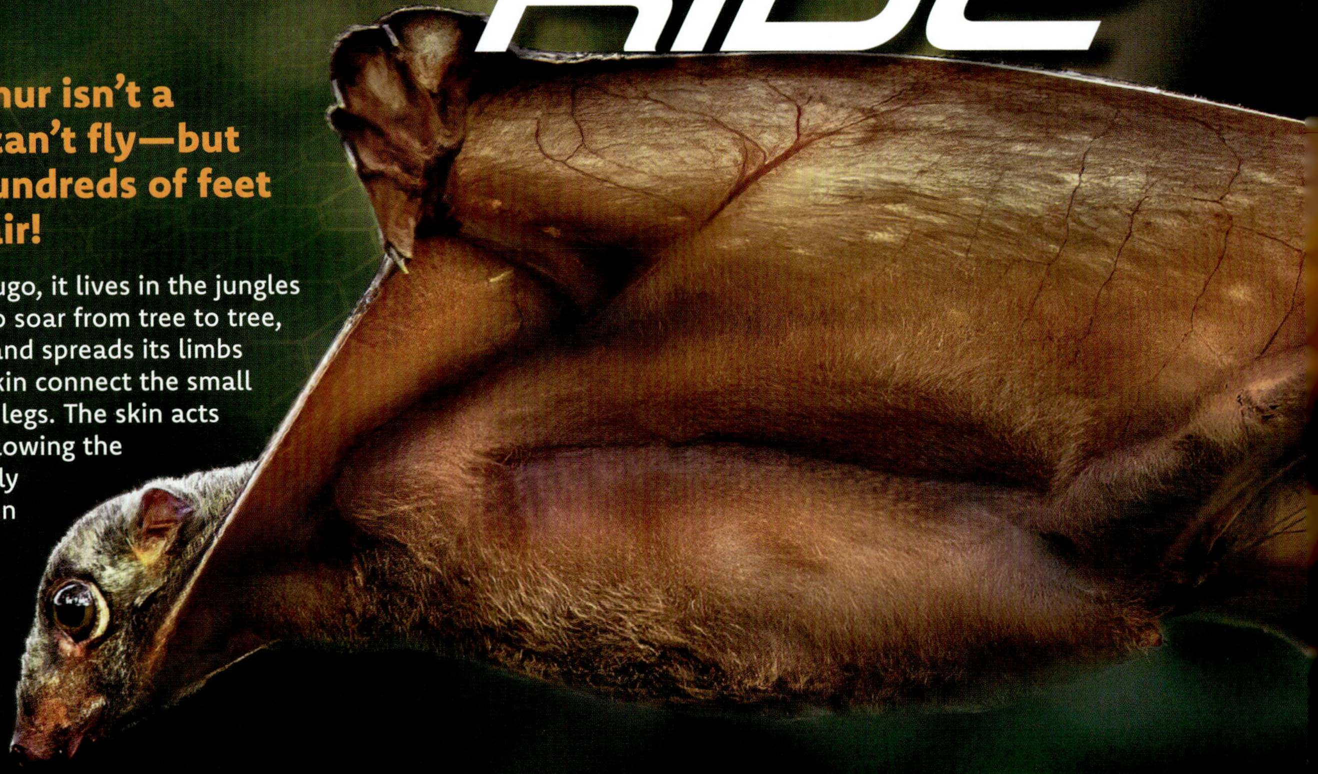

The flying lemur isn't a lemur and it can't fly—but it can glide hundreds of feet through the air!

Also known as a colugo, it lives in the jungles of Southeast Asia. To soar from tree to tree, it leaps into the air and spreads its limbs out. Large flaps of skin connect the small mammal's arms and legs. The skin acts like a hang glider, allowing the colugo to glide swiftly through the air. When hanging out in the trees, a mother colugo can also use her skin flaps like a pouch to hold her baby!

Storm Suckers

In the mid-1800s, English doctor George Merryweather came up with an odd way to predict storms—using leeches! Back in George's day, doctors often kept live leeches in jars to treat patients. George noticed that when storms neared, the leeches would sometimes move higher up in their jars. George used this instinct to make his "Tempest Prognosticator"—which is just a fancy way of saying "storm predictor." He put 12 jars, each with one leech inside, in a circle. Each jar was connected to a bell with a chain. When the leeches moved high enough, they would make the bells ring. A lot of ringing meant a bad storm was likely!

FACT FILES

A baby colugo clings to its mother's belly for the first few months of its life, even while she's gliding!

Twig Trickster

The buff-tip moth looks just like a broken twig! The moth is a master of disguise when it pulls its wings close to its body. The moth's brown and gray color blends in with its surroundings. During the day, the moth can be found sitting on a twig or on the ground, where it remains undetected by predators. At night, it comes alive and flutters around in search of food.

COLOR SENSE ↗ Butterflies can see colors that humans can't. They have hundreds of eyes, or lenses, whereas humans only have two. Their enhanced vision lets them see millions of shades, including ultraviolet. Their supersense helps them find nectar to feed on from different kinds of flowers.

LONELY SUNFISH ↗ A solitary sunfish lost its appetite when its aquarium was temporarily closed to visitors. Keepers at the Kaikyokan Aquarium in Japan realized that the fish was feeling lonely, so they placed life-size human cutouts outside the tank and dressed them up in their uniforms. The next morning the fish ate for the first time in a week.

SNAKE FEAR ↗ A newly discovered species of Peruvian snake was named after actor Harrison Ford. On screen he played Indiana Jones, who is terrified of snakes. An extreme fear of snakes is called ophidiophobia.

ALWAYS ALERT ↗ Ducks often sleep with one eye open. This helps them detect danger, even while dozing.

Hummingbird HOSPITAL

Catia Lattouf turned her apartment in Mexico City into a hummingbird hospital!

The 75-year-old set up the clinic in 2012, after she nursed an injured hummingbird back to health. Now she cares for hundreds of these tiny birds every year. Some of them are injured or sick. Others are just very young and still unable to look after themselves properly. The birds start in her bedroom, where they get round-the-clock care. When they're well enough to fly and feed from nectar drippers, they move to the next room. When the time is right, they're set free in a local wooded area.

Catia Lattouf

COUNTING FISH ↗ Clownfish, the stars of *Finding Nemo*, can count up to three. They use this skill to count the number of white stripes on other fish. That way they can decide whether it is a friendly fish of another species or a rival clownfish. Common clownfish have three stripes and fiercely guard their territory from other clownfish. So they are most likely to attack fish with the same number of stripes as themselves.

PUZZLING BEHAVIOR ↗ Lambeau, a mixed breed dog from North Carolina, had to be treated by a veterinarian after eating more than 250 jigsaw puzzle pieces.

Helicoptor Attack

Australian wedge-tailed eagles jealously guard their territory. They will attack drones, paragliders, and even helicopters that fly too close.

CANNIBAL MOTHERS ↗ If they are feeling stressed, female hamsters sometimes eat their young. They may also devour their offspring if they are extremely hungry or if they think their babies are under threat.

LUCKY DOG ↗ A fluffy Pomeranian dog named Paris miraculously survived a fall from the 12th floor of an apartment building in Colombia. And there wasn't even a scratch on her! The little dog plunged more than 100 feet (30.5 m) and crashed through the corrugated iron roof of a three-story building next door. Her owner spotted her pet through a hole in the roof made by her fall.

Wistful Thinking

At Kawachi Garden in Japan, you can wander through roughly 330-foot-long (100.6-m) flower-filled tunnels! In springtime, flowers bloom as far as the eye can see. Purple and white wisteria flowers from more than 150 vines tumble from the top. As the light shines through, people feel like they're in a dream!

RIPLEY'S COLLECTION

EXHIBIT NO. 18010

White Spines

Found in Montana, this porcupine survived into adulthood despite nature working against it. The bright white color causes the animal to stand out, making it an easy target for predators. Not only that, but its quills are also softer than normal and thus offer less protection. This had to be one tough critter!

SOFT QUILLS, TOUGH PORCUPINE!

SEE MORE!

NATURAL WONDERS

SPIDER SPINES

Spiny orb weavers have a foolproof way of making themselves seem less appetizing to birds or lizards—long, shiny spines!

These long, shiny spines are only found on female spiny orb weavers. The females are much easier to spot because they are brighter and bigger than the males—up to 10 times their size, in fact! And they don't like to move around too much, spending most of their time on their circular webs, waiting for a snack to pass by. Easy prey, right? Wrong! The spines on some species can measure up to 2 inches (5.1 cm) long, letting a predator know that this is no easy meal.

EXTINCT SNAKE ↗ Researchers in India unearthed the remains of a gigantic extinct snake, *Vasuki indicus*, that lived 47 million years ago. It measured almost 50 feet (15.3 m) in length—longer than a school bus and nearly twice the length of the longest reticulated python ever recorded—and weighed around 1 ton.

SURFBOARD SNATCH ↗ During the summer of 2023, a female sea otter snatched several surfboards from surfers off the coast of Santa Cruz, California.

FEATHERED FRIENDS ↗ Since 1664, it has been illegal to insult a swan in Hamburg, Germany.

WET WEATHER ↗ Seattle, Washington, has a reputation for wet weather. But it gets at least 30 percent less annual rainfall than Houston, Texas.

GIANT GAP ↗ The time difference between the existence of *Stegosaurus* and *Tyrannosaurus rex* is greater than that between *Tyrannosaurus rex* and the smartphone. The two dinos did not walk the Earth during the same time. *Stegosaurus* roamed the planet around 80–100 million years before *T. rex*, which itself lived about 66 million years ago.

CROW CONFUSION ↗ A crow singing in a tree in Oxfordshire, England, learned to mimic the sound of two-tone police car sirens. At first, Thames Valley police officers believed their sirens were faulty.

HUGE HIVE ↗ A huge hive containing up to 65,000 honeybees was found in the attic of Ashley Massis Class's 100-year-old farmhouse in North Carolina. It had taken the bees eight months to build the hive, which extended down the wall of her three-year-old daughter Saylor's bedroom. The beekeeper who was called out to deal with the problem removed 100 pounds (45.4 kg) of honeycomb.

METAL NESTS ↗ To keep birds away from buildings, some cities erect anti-bird spikes. In parts of Europe, crows and magpies have been stealing the strips of sharp metal to add to their nests.

DEITY DIGITS ↗ When Sarju Devi gave birth in 2023 to a healthy girl with 14 fingers and 12 toes in Bharatpur, India, her family proclaimed the baby to be the reincarnation of a Hindu goddess, Dhologarh Devi, who is depicted in statues as a young girl with several arms.

Silky Snare

Found in Australia, a whip spider might be mistaken for a worm—with legs! It's thought the long body is actually meant to make the spider look like a tiny twig. This clever camouflage is part of a top-notch trap. First, the whip spider weaves a few silk strands between leaves. It then waits on one of these strands, looking like a small branch that got caught on the web. An unsuspecting wandering spider crosses this "handy" bridge, and before they know it, they're wrapped in a sticky silk bundle, ready for snack time. Game over.

Something Shady

It's not uncommon to see a spider web or two on a lampshade (especially one that hasn't been dusted in a while). But a spider web in the shape of a lampshade? That's another story! The lampshade spider spins a web that looks like it should be on top of a lamp. The unique shape allows the spider to catch prey that flies too close. The spider makes its intricate web under rock formations and in caves. This clever arachnid can be found in parts of the U.S. and in China.

Tufa Towers

Mono Lake in California grows its own towers! Beneath the lake's surface, salty minerals from nearby mountains react with calcium from springs under the lake. The result? Solid limestone called "tufa." Over hundreds of years, the tufa builds up into towers that can reach up to 30 feet (9.1 m) tall! Some of the tufa towers in Mono Lake are more than 13,000 years old. Tufa can only grow underwater. When water was drained from the lake in the 1940s, it left many towers visible on the shore. People from around the world visit Mono Lake to see these strange formations!

The water in Mono Lake is 2.5 times as salty as the ocean!

RESCUE RUN ↗ A dog named Blue ran 4 miles (6.4 km) to fetch help after owner Brandon Garrett crashed into a ravine in Baker County, Oregon. When Blue arrived at the family's campsite with cuts on his snout, Garrett's family suspected there had been an accident. They launched a search and when they found the overturned truck the next morning, they heard Garrett calling for help a short distance away. Thanks to Blue, he sustained nothing worse than some cuts, bruises, and a foot injury.

GIANT RAT ↗ The Vangunu giant rat from the Solomon Islands is more than twice the size of a common rat, and it can crack open coconuts with its strong teeth.

SMALL SKATER ↗ Li Jiangtao has taught his cat, Bao Zi, to ride a skateboard. He originally got the cat to deal with a rodent infestation, but when he was training his dog on a skateboard, Bao Zi seemed interested. It took about a year for the cat to master the art.

BARNYARD BREW

To celebrate the Chinese New Year in February 2024, the Shanghai branch of Starbucks introduced a limited-edition latte flavored like braised pork. The savory coffee was seasoned with pork sauce and topped with a piece of cooked pork meat.

GUARD GEESE ↗ In 2023, a prison in Santa Catarina, Brazil, replaced its guard dogs with a flock of geese to patrol the space between the prison's inner fence and its outer wall. As well as being cheaper than dogs and equally noisy, geese are more vigilant.

HARMFUL HORNET ↗ Asian giant hornets prey on bees, and a single hornet can kill 40 honeybees in one minute by using its huge, powerful jaw to decapitate its victims. Known as the "murder hornet," it also possesses a sting deadly enough to kill 10 mice.

SAINT PANCAKE ↗ Every year on November 29, residents of Rotterdam in the Netherlands wear pancakes on their heads to celebrate the fictional Sint Pannekoek (Saint Pancake). The celebration was invented in 1986 by Dutch cartoonist Jan Kruis.

THAT'S NUTS!

Believe it or not, this isn't a forest—it's one big tree!

The world's largest cashew tree is just south of Natal, Brazil. It covers 2 acres. That's about the size of two football fields! The tree grows so big thanks to a genetic mutation. Unlike most cashew trees, its branches spread sideways, touch the ground, and grow new roots. It's thought to be more than 100 years old and still makes lots of fruit and nuts. People in Brazil especially love cashew apples, the sweet fruit that grows above each nut!

Left: A view from above of Brazil's giant cashew tree. Above: A close-up of a cashew fruit and nut.

Shell Secret

If you see a shell moving on the beach, it might be a granulate shellback crab! This crafty crab finds an empty seashell, then uses its rear legs to hold itself inside. The shell acts like a shield, helping the crab hide from hungry predators. The crab learns this lifesaving technique when it is young. At first it's too small for a full shell, so it uses shell fragments instead.

LOST STRIPES ↗ In places where skunks face fewer enemies, their distinctive black-and-white stripes often fade or disappear. This process is called "relaxed selection." Where they are not at risk from coyotes or mountain lions, skunks don't need the warning signal that their stripes provide.

SURVIVAL RATE ↗ Only 5 percent of cheetah cubs in the wild reach adulthood. Many cubs are killed by lions or hyenas.

THIEVING SEAGULL ↗ A seagull was banned from a store in Dorset, England, for stealing potato chips. The bird made off with about 30 bags of chips over the course of a two-month crime spree. By that point, it had been regularly stealing from the shop for six years.

KANGAROO AMBUSH ↗ An Australian man suffered serious injuries after being attacked by a massive kangaroo. The kangaroo stood 6.5 feet (2 m) tall and weighed about 220 pounds (99.8 kg). The man crossed its path while walking from his house in Willows, Queensland, to his car. He was flown to the hospital with deep cuts on his hip, arms, and chest.

FREE TRAVEL ↗ Tilly the cat hopped on a train and traveled just about 18 miles (29 km) to London, England, without her owner. The South Western Railway company were so impressed that they presented Tilly with her own railcard. This allows her to travel free by train for the rest of her life.

DELAYED WIN ↗ In 2024, Bobby Allison won a NASCAR Cup Series race—53 years after it had taken place. A cup car is a special type of NASCAR vehicle, and Bobby was not driving a cup car when he won at Bowman Gray Stadium in North Carolina in 1971. Thus his victory was never recognized as a Cup Series win, and for more than half a century that race did not have an official winner. At age 86, Bobby was finally awarded his 85th victory in the series.

IRON TEETH ↗ Komodo dragons easily rip through the flesh of deer or water buffalo. Its strong teeth are coated with a thin layer of iron along the tips and cutting edges. The iron gives the teeth an orange color. In its mouth are about 60 serrated teeth, each up to 1 inch (2.5 cm) long. Luckily they never have to see a dentist!

Building Blocks

The male river chub is an underwater architect, building a giant nest out of rocks. The fish fetches the rocks in its mouth—sometimes from 75 feet (22.9 m) away! It does this all to impress a mate. Tens of thousands of rocks later, he's built a giant mound on the riverbed. The nest can end up several feet across. The rocky pile is a safe spot for the female to lay eggs. The river chub is one hard worker!

SOLAR SLUG

This sea slug powers itself with energy from the sun—just like a plant!

Sometimes called a leaf slug or a sea sheep, it is one of the only animals that can photosynthesize. It eats algae and stores special energy-making cells inside its body. All the slug has to do to make more energy is go out into the sun! The "leaf sheep" is tiny—smaller than your fingernail. With a white face, black eyes, and green leaf-like growths called cerata, this little slug blends in easily with its coral reef home.

FACT FILES

Photosynthesis is how plants make their own food using sunlight, water, and carbon dioxide.

MATURE MOUNDS A series of active termite mounds along the Buffels River in Namaqualand, South Africa, are 34,000 years old and date back to when woolly mammoths roamed the planet.

PRESIDENTIAL PETS Former U.S. president Calvin Coolidge was given twin lion cubs as a gift by the mayor of Johannesburg, South Africa. Coolidge named them Tax Reduction and Budget Bureau.

PENGUIN PROBLEM In January 2024, an airplane was delayed from taking off at New Zealand's Wellington International Airport because of a blue penguin on the runway. The pilot and passengers waited until the bird was escorted to safety by airport staff.

FANCY FEATHER

A single feather from an extinct huia bird, the last confirmed sighting of which occurred in 1907, sold at a 2024 auction in New Zealand for more than $28,000. The huia was considered sacred by the Māori people.

TOILET TRAUMA A woman in Moscow, Russia, was horrified to see a boa constrictor hanging out of the toilet bowl in her bathroom. The albino snake, which belonged to another resident in the same building, had slithered down its owner's bathtub drain and worked its way along the pipes before appearing in the woman's toilet bowl.

PERPETUAL PREGNANCY Frilled sharks can be pregnant for up to 3.5 years before giving birth to their pups.

CROC CONTEST On the same day as the famous Melbourne Cup horse race in Australia, the Berry Springs Tavern stages a crocodile race. Young saltwater crocs race along a track of fake grass, which is lined with hay bales to keep them running straight ahead.

Dry Eye

In the middle of the Sahara, there's a 30-mile-wide (48.3-km) eye! Known as the "Eye of the Sahara," it looks like lots of circles carved into the rock. Scientists once thought it was a crater made by a meteor. However, they now believe it first formed from a bubble of hot magma. Then, over time, wind and rain wore down parts of the rock into concentric circles. An amazing natural beauty!

VIEW FROM OUTER SPACE!

FIERY FEATHERS

In the winter of 2025, bird watchers in Huron County, Michigan, spotted a colorful surprise: an orange owl!

Snowy owls are named for their white feathers, which help them blend in with the winter landscape. But this bird, nicknamed "Creamsicle" by photographer Julie Maggert, can't help but stand out. The cause of its orange feathers is a mystery. Some experts think Creamsicle was born that way. Others say the color might be dye or paint. We may never know the reason behind Creamsicle's flamboyant feathers—since the bird seems healthy, there are no plans to capture it and find out!

OWL WITH ORANGE FEATHERS!

RIPLEY'S COLLECTION

EXHIBIT NO. 18209

Sticky Situation

Millions of years ago, a pair of insects landed on a tree in what is now Russia. Some sticky resin leaked from the plant and trapped the tiny creatures. Over time, the resin fossilized into amber. This preserved the insects, leaving us with an up-close view of prehistoric life frozen in time!

MAMMOTH WITH A MANE!

EXHIBIT NO. 176204

Stylish Skull

This woolly mammoth skull is small but amazing. The skull most likely came from a juvenile. It even still has some of its hair intact! The woolly mammoth walked the Earth hundreds of thousands of years ago, traveling in herds, before going extinct.

TINY TUSKS!

SEE MORE!

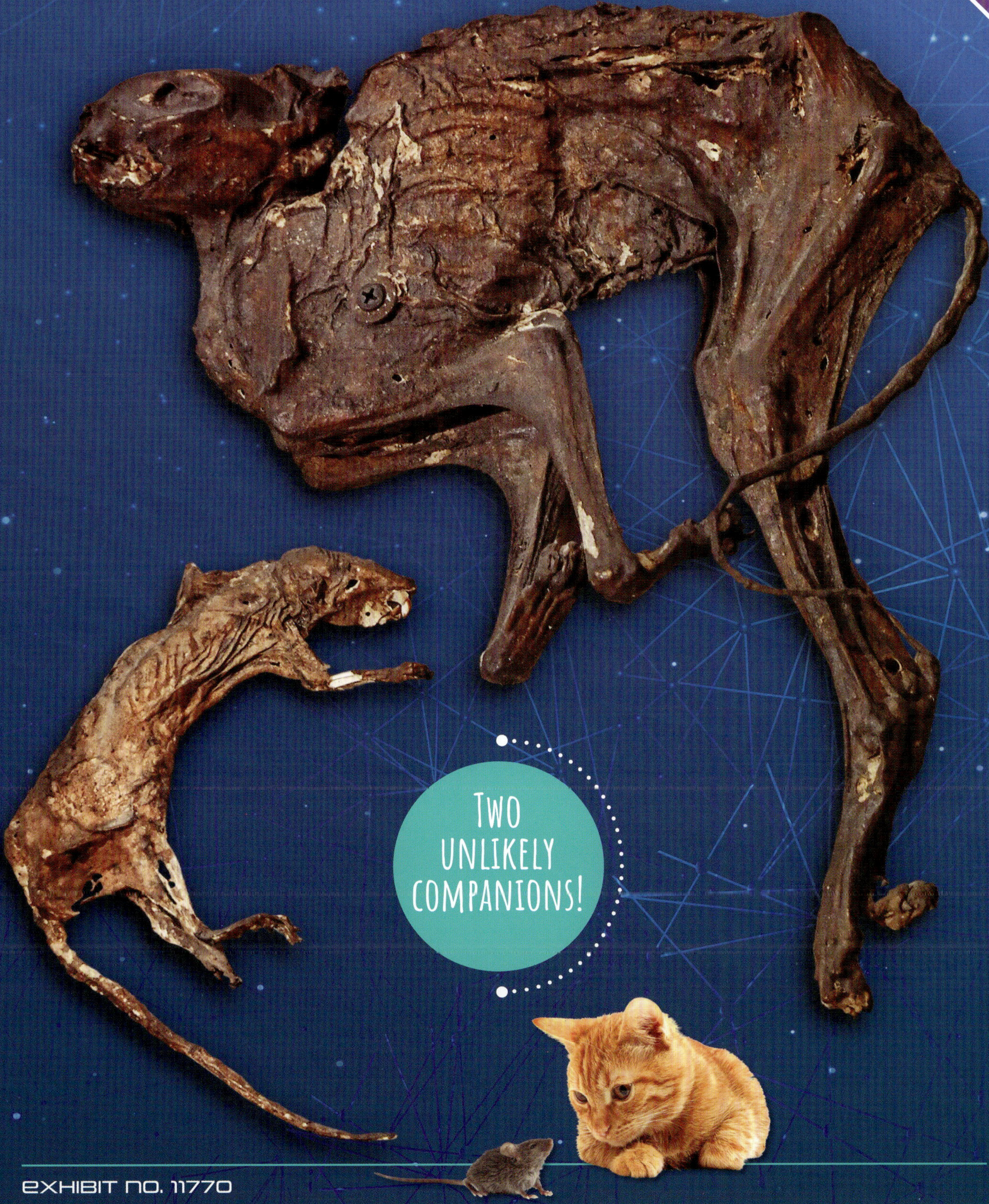

TWO UNLIKELY COMPANIONS!

EXHIBIT NO. 11770

Ghost Guardians

This mummified cat and rat was found hidden inside the walls of a sixteenth-century house in Exeter, England. Believe it or not, the remains were stored there on purpose! Long ago, people made "foundation sacrifices." They believed the spirit of the animals would protect the house from bad luck and evil forces.

UP NEXT...

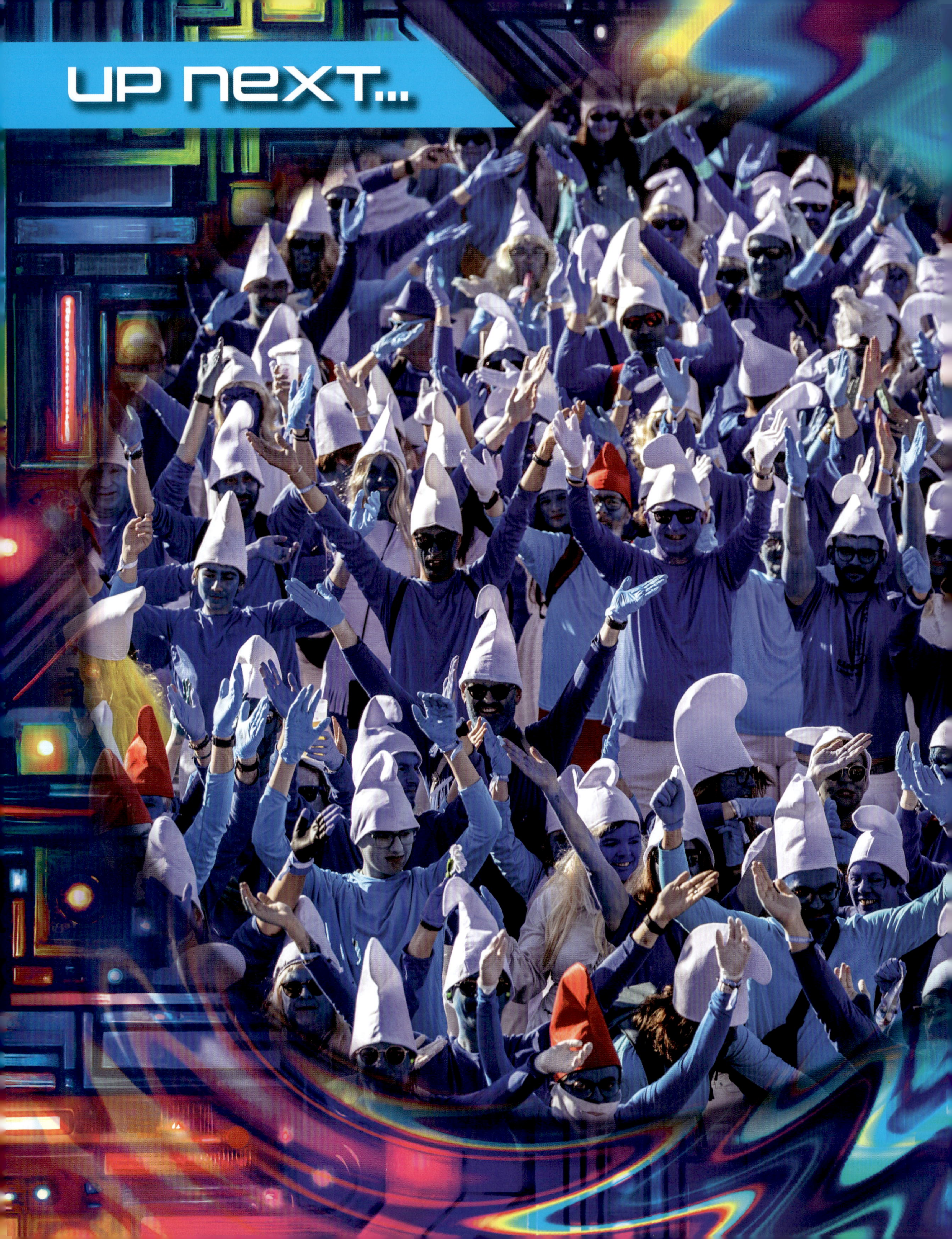

POP
CULTURE

SMURF Swarm

In May 2025, a small town in France was flooded in a sea of blue—not of water, but of people dressed as Smurfs!

The colorful bunch gathered on a sunny day in the town of Landerneau, dressed from head to foot in Smurf costumes. With 3,076 participants, it was the largest known gathering of people dressed as the little blue characters. The Smurfs were wearing white or red hats, blue tops, and white trousers. The Smurfettes were clad in white dresses, white hats, and yellow wigs. And Smurfs were not only face-painted but also body-painted in blue!

Saddled-up Swifties

Taylor Swift's Eras tour was loved by millions of fans—including horses! Many people wore friendship bracelets for the concerts. The bracelets showed song lyrics or album names. When Taylor performed in Toronto and Vancouver, hundreds of thousands of people showed up. Police on horseback helped control the crowds. Their horses even joined in on the fun by wearing giant friendship bracelets on their necks!

Wearing Waste

Eco-designers VIN + OMI, from the UK, are changing trash into high-end fashion. They want to show that we can use our waste more wisely—because we can wear it! So far, they have made fabrics from things like ocean plastic and old wet suits. They have even made "leather" from old milk cartons. But the designers didn't stop there. What about natural waste? They're on it, with garments made from garden cuttings and wood chippings!

CLOTHES MADE FROM TRASH!

SUBWAY SLEEPER ↗ Before he became successful, UK musician Ed Sheeran used to catch up on his sleep after a late-night gig by going round and round on Circle Line subway trains in London from 5:00 a.m. until noon.

WEAPON FEST ↗ There are more than one billion usable weapons in the video game *Borderlands 3.*

EIFFEL ENEMY ↗ Nineteenth-century French writer Guy de Maupassant hated the newly built Eiffel Tower so much that he used to eat lunch every day at the restaurant in the base of the tower—because it was one of the few places in Paris from where he could not see the famous landmark.

TIGHT BUDGET ↗ For their work on *Dallas Buyers Club*, Adruitha Lee and Robin Mathews won the 2014 Academy Award for Best Makeup and Hairstyling, even though the film's makeup budget was only $250.

RARE ENGRAVING ↗ In 2011, 11-year-old Mat Winter discovered an elaborate engraving at a dumpsite in Kent, England. He kept it at home for more than a decade before deciding to have it valued. It turned out to be a more than 500-year-old woodcut by German Renaissance artist Albrecht Dürer. In 2024, it sold at auction for around $44,000.

PRIVATE PREP ↗ Australian actor Heath Ledger hid himself away in a hotel room for about a month to prepare for his role as the Joker in the movie *The Dark Knight.*

SHAKESPEAREAN SAYING ↗ The phrase "good riddance" was popularized by William Shakespeare's early seventeenth-century play *Troilus and Cressida.*

DUSTY Designs

Designer Rahat Rai turned household dust into a pair of slippers!

But where did he get the dust? From vacuum cleaners, of course! It sounds completely made up, but Rahat did just that. He was a student at Ravensbourne University in London when he came up with an idea. He wanted to turn this overlooked waste material into something new and useful. Rahat gathered the dust, heated it to kill germs, and pressed it to make a fabric strong enough to wear. The end result? Eco-friendly footwear!

PADDINGTON PASSPORT ↗ Britain's Home Office issued an official passport for fictional character Paddington Bear. The producers of the 2024 film *Paddington in Peru* asked for a replica passport to use in the movie. Instead, the Home Office provided an official one, including Paddington's photo, date, and place of birth, and listing him simply as Bear.

EXPENSIVE CHEETO ↗ A Flamin' Hot Cheeto sold at auction for $87,840! The 3-inch-long (7.5-cm) Cheeto attracted 60 bids. It was popular at the auction because the shape resembled the dragon-like Pokémon Charizard.

ISLAND PURCHASE ↗ Mystery author Alexander McCall Smith used the royalties from his books to buy a chain of islands. He paid more than $409,000 to purchase the uninhabited islands off the coast of his native Scotland. His aim was to ensure that they will always remain a safe place for wildlife.

150 VERSES ↗ Canadian singer-songwriter Leonard Cohen wrote 150 draft verses for his song "Hallelujah." It took him five years to write. He often performed different versions of the song during his concerts.

Carved Coats

British sculptor Tom Waugh carves full-sized coats from marble! It takes him weeks to transform the lumps of marble. Using traditional tools—and lots of patience—he carves every crease, curve, and fold into the soft stone. The end result looks like a real winter coat hanging on a hook. Tom's sculptures are so convincing that you might mistakenly try to pick one up and wear it. But if you did, you'd quickly realize the solid stone won't budge!

Tom Waugh

FROM OLD JEANS TO NEW PURSE!

Handbag Houses

Zach Frisbie uses scrap material to make bags that look like buildings! The purse designer from Los Angeles learned to sew when he was 19 years old. He only uses waste material, like old jeans. He designed a haunted house duffel bag that took 775 hours to complete, including his time testing out ideas. It sold for nearly $28,000!

Zach Frisbie

Labubu Love

Tennis legend Naomi Osaka brought some special friends with her to the 2025 U.S. Open—Labubu dolls covered in crystals! The dolls were custom-made by artist Kerin Rose Gold. Each one took her between 8 and 12 hours to make. Naomi named the bedazzled dolls after other famous tennis players, and she also gave each Labubu a little tennis racket!

THESE DOLLS HAVE SWAG!

LABUBU LOWDOWN

Some Labubu fans get **tattoos and piercings** for their dolls!

You can meet a **Labubu** at the theme park **POPLAND,** located in **Beijing, China.**

All Labubus are **female elf-like creatures** that are mischievous.

Labubus were created by **Hong Kong artist Kasing Lung.**

Their popularity has spawned **fake dolls,** which fans call **"lafufus."**

The creatures **first appeared** in the 2015 book series ***The Monsters.***

A real Labubu doll has **nine pointy teeth.**

Dough Doll

One House Bakery in California baked a 7-foot-tall (2.1 m) Labubu out of bread! They named it LeVanVan, after the levain used to make the dough. The huge sculpture weighed about 300 pounds (136.1 kg) and needed a wooden frame for support. Every piece was shaped and baked by hand. The challenge was splitting the character into pieces small enough for their oven!

POP CULTURE

Mini Manicure

Hazel Maradey gives Labubu dolls a glow-up with pretty press-on nails!

Hazel is a nail artist from Illinois. She normally does nail art for humans. But in early 2025, she was asked to make nails for a Labubu doll. She tried and it was a success! Now Hazel makes all sorts of little Labubu nail designs. To make the tiny nails, Hazel shapes slivers of acrylic. They are around just 0.08 inches (0.2 cm) wide! Then she uses pointed tweezers and a super-fine paintbrush to decorate them.

A *Stitch* IN TIME

Creative crafter Sophie O'Neill, from Glasgow, UK, keeps a journal made of stitches!

On January 1, 2020, Sophie started a daily journal. But she didn't write in a book—she sewed a symbol onto some fabric. The symbol was a fountain full of confetti, which she had seen after a New Year's party. Sophie adds a new symbol to the diary for each day. She has stitched things like a cup of coffee, a Christmas stocking, and even a tissue for when she was sick!

ONE ICON STITCHED PER DAY!

Dirty Dozen

Andy Bailey from Cheshire, UK, found beauty in local trash cans—so much that he turned it into a calendar! Over the course of a year, he photographed around 130 different trash cans. Andy even made a scoring system! So far, no trash can has received a perfect score. The trashy calendar is for a good cause, as Andy donates a portion of the sales to a local charity.

TRASH CANS GET NAMED AND RATED!

HAPPY BIRTHDAY ↗ Blower is a smartphone app that lets you blow out the candles on a birthday cake with your phone. The app pushes out air through the phone's speaker holes.

GAMING GLOVES ↗ So many joystick hand blisters were reported by children in America playing *Mario Party* that Nintendo offered protective sports gloves to families that purchased a copy of the video game.

BACKWARD BASES ↗ On June 23, 1963, the New York Mets' outfielder Jimmy Piersall celebrated the 100th home run of his career by running the bases facing backward.

RAILWAY RUN ↗ Tackling one line a day and sometimes battling temperatures of nearly 90°F (32.2°C), ultramarathoner Jonny Davies ran the entire length of the London Underground train network in 11 days, covering 354 miles (569.7 km).

1,001 CHEESES ↗ French pizza chefs Benoît Bruel and Fabien Montellanico teamed up with cheesemaker Sophie Hatat Richart-Luna to create a pizza topped with 1,001 different varieties of cheese—940 of them from France.

HOLES-IN-ONE ↗ Beating odds of 17 million to one, golfers Steve Spina and Chuck LaVarnway hit back-to-back holes-in-one at Andalusia Country Club in California on September 23, 2023.

Pooping Pooches

Jake Wagenman of California makes a calendar each year showing dogs going number two! Twelve lucky pooches are picked to receive the squatting honor. Each image shows a dog doing their thing in a scenic spot. It is not all fun and games. All that poo goes toward a good cause! A portion of each sale is donated to the Maui Humane Society.

MIXED MEDIA

Australian artist Jensen Dean paints celebrities using objects like dolls, dumbbells, and knives!

Why the odd tools? Jensen picks them based on his subjects. He painted boxer Mike Tyson using boxing gloves. With a knife, he painted chef Gordon Ramsay. And he brought movie star Margot Robbie to life with Barbie dolls, celebrating her role in the *Barbie* movie! Jensen used a Barbie doll's hair and feet to paint the famous actress! Jensen's technique may be unique, but his paintings are instantly recognizable.

GORDON RAMSAY

ARNOLD SCHWARZENEGGER

SEE MORE!

RIPLEY'S COLLECTION

THIS IS THE WAY!

EXHIBIT NO. 176251

Hero's Helmet

This helmet was worn by actor Pedro Pascal in season one of *The Mandalorian*. He played the main character, Din Djarin. He wears the helmet for almost the entire show! It hides his face and adds mystery to every scene. Today it is one of the most famous helmets in the Star Wars universe.

Musical Mice

Welcome to Mouse Fest 2025 with "Nibbles and the Nuts!" Photographer Simon Dell from Sheffield, England, turned an area of his yard into a music fest for mice. He included a tiny stage, instruments, and a snack bar. He photographed the mice as they explored the area. One curious mouse even got behind the drum kit. Simon created his mouse village back in 2018 and is always adding to it.

THESE RODENTS ROCK!

ROTTEN REVIEWS ↗ Chinese amateur historian Zhuang Tinglong's unauthorized story of the country's Ming dynasty was not popular. It was so poorly received in 1660 that more than 70 people associated with the book's publication were executed.

RIVAL ATTRACTION ↗ When The Beatles played in Dingwall, Scotland, in January 1963, there were only 19 people in the audience. A local band, The Melotones, were playing nearby on the same night and drew a crowd of over 1,000.

BUNK BEDS ↗ Be careful how you sleep! Every year in the United States, around 71,000 people are treated in hospital emergency rooms as a result of accidents involving bunk beds.

FLYING HIPPOS

Hippos can fly. They run so fast, they can become totally airborne for up to 0.3 seconds at a time. Since all four feet are briefly off the ground while they are running at full speed, technically they are flying!

VALUABLE LESSON ↗ Arsenal Football Club manager Mikel Arteta once hired professional pickpockets to steal phones and wallets from his players while they dined together. The idea was to teach them the importance of being constantly alert and prepared.

BUSY BURGLAR ↗ A very tidy burglar broke into a house in Wales. The thief hung the homeowner's laundry up to dry, cleaned the floor, put the groceries away, and refilled the bird feeders.

HOME PRISON ↗ At the end of World War II, Japanese general Hitoshi Imamura was sentenced to 10 years' imprisonment for war crimes. But he thought the sentence was too lenient, so he built a replica prison cell in his yard and stayed in it until his death in 1968.

Pocket-Sized PUPS

Japanese artist Terumi Ohta creates lifelike dogs out of wool!

Terumi brings the furry creations to life with a single felting needle. Each pup is small enough to fit in the palm of your hand. But that doesn't mean they're quick to make! She spends hundreds of hours on each sculpture! The pups have playful expressions and realistic fur that is fun to pet. Terumi is self-taught and started making sculptures in 2012. In addition to her signature wool dogs, she also creates cats and wolves. She even crafted a tiny elephant!

NOT REAL DOGS!

Wiggin' OUT!

Lexus Lewis of Augusta, Georgia, makes wigs out of balloons!

Lexus made her first balloon wig for her 27th birthday. She has made one every year since then. To create her unique looks, she mixes colors, lengths, and types of balloons. She even curls some of them! As an artist, Lexus often uses objects in unexpected ways. She loves balloons because they can have so many different meanings. Besides wigs, she's also used them for things like clothing, paintings, and sculptures!

PUT YOUR PARTY WIG ON!

Lexus Lewis

Forest Friends

Thomas Dambo from Denmark turns timber into towering trolls! The artist builds magnificent giants from scrap wood and recycled materials. Some of his trolls stand nearly 40 feet (12.2 m) tall, with friendly faces and silly poses that look straight out of a fairy tale. With the help of volunteers, each statue takes about 750 hours to complete. So far, there are 170 of these fun works of art around the world.

CLOSE-UP OF THE FEATHERS!

Cartoon Chicken

The Sebright chicken is kind of sketchy—in a good way! Its feathers look like someone has drawn around them with a black pen. The dark outlines make the gold or silvery-white feathers appear cartoon-like. Both males and females share the same amazing look. These living works of art are usually bred to be show birds.

STARRY SANCTUARY

In Mount Dora, Florida, a house has been completely painted in the style of van Gogh's *Starry Night!*

Nancy Nemhauser and Ludomir Jastrzebski hired an artist to paint the outside walls of their home. They love the famous bright blue and gold swirls. It helps their son Chip, who has autism, find his way home. *Starry Night* is his favorite painting! When city officials ordered them to remove the murals, Nancy and Ludomir fought back—and won. Now their colorful house is a star tourist attraction!

TOP *This!*

Nick Yatsinko of Phoenix, Arizona, turns pizza into art you can eat!

Nick's slices stand out from other pizza art thanks to his unique technique. He uses food coloring to paint right onto the cheese! That way he can create just about anything—cartoons, celebrities, and more! Nick always loved art, so he started painting pizzas to attract more customers into his restaurant. It worked! Now people ask him to make custom "master-pizzas" that are almost too cool to eat.

Nick Yatsinko

CHEESY CHARIZARD CREATION!

A TRUE MASTER-PIZZA TREAT!

POP CULTURE

Edible ATTIRE

Anne Wold of Los Angeles, California, makes fashion out of food—including pretzel chain mail!

Ever since she went to art college, Anne has enjoyed working with unusual materials for her pieces. She tried using food, dollar-store stuff, and trash. Along with a skirt, she's also made purses out of pretzel chain mail. She even made a dress out of 2,400 beans, drilling a small hole in each bean and then linking them all together into a dress shape. It can take from a few days to a few months for her to finish each garment.

Bean dress

Coffee dress

Pretzel chain-mail skirt

Cereal purse

FILM FIGURINES ↗ Australian Steele Harris-Walker has collected more than 1,000 Funko Pop! vinyl figurines depicting celebrities and characters from TV and film, including *Star Wars*, *Stranger Things*, and *Harry Potter*.

FIRST REMOTE ↗ Launched in 1950, the first TV remote control, the Zenith Lazy Bones, was connected to the TV by a cable.

CAREER CHANGE ↗ Child actor Peter Ostrum's only film role was as Charlie Bucket in the 1971 movie *Willy Wonka and the Chocolate Factory*. After that, he gave up acting and became a veterinarian in Lowville, New York.

ROADSIDE RUST ↗ Australian farmer Jim Sauer created an art installation featuring more than a dozen pieces of rusty machinery—including cars, trucks, bikes, a boat, a plane, and a bulldozer—perched atop wooden power poles and spaced out along the roadside in Queensland. He hopes to add a helicopter someday.

LUCKY LANDING

In September 2023, a climber miraculously survived a 1,968-foot (599.9-m) fall from near the summit of New Zealand's treacherous Mount Taranaki. Despite plunging the equivalent of a 200-story building, he escaped with only minor injuries because he landed in a patch of soft snow.

MADONNA MARKINGS ↗ Tara Berry, of Kansas, has 18 tattoos of Madonna on her body, with images spanning the singer's entire career. She got her first in 2016, and her tattoos include Madonna's famous kiss with Britney Spears at the 2003 MTV Video Music Awards.

BRAIN BULLET ↗ Brazilian medical student Mateus Facio partied for four days with a bullet lodged in his brain. He didn't even realize that he had been shot. He thought he had been hit by a stone at a New Year's Eve beach party near Rio de Janeiro.

NASAL NASTIES ↗ A man in Jacksonville, Florida, had 150 live larval bugs removed from his nose by doctors. The bugs were feeding on the inside of his nose, causing him to suffer constant nosebleeds and swelling in his face and lips.

FAST TYPIST ↗ SK Ashraf, a lawyer from India, typed the English alphabet backward from Z to A on a laptop keyboard in only 2.88 seconds.

Bougie Bread

Swedish designer Gustaf Westman made a bag that can only carry a single baguette! Gustaf debuted the must-have accessory for his Paris pop-up shop in 2025. It was made in Stockholm out of recycled plastic. The bold piece cradles a crusty loaf as though it's a luxury item. Like many fashion statements, the bright pink spiral is not meant to be practical. But in a city famous for both fashion and food, it makes sense to carry the iconic bread in a truly chic way!

RIB CROWN ↗ Emily James from Missouri spent $17,000 to have six of her ribs removed. She wanted to have a smaller waist. After the surgery, she announced that she was going to turn the removed ribs into a crown.

EXPERIENCED BARBER ↗ Shitsui Hakoishi was still working as a barber in Japan at age 108. Her career spanned nine decades. She got her barber's license when she was 18 and established a salon in her hometown of Nakagawa in 1953.

WASTED JOURNEY ↗ Golden Lion, a soccer team from the tiny Caribbean island of Martinique, made an 8,000-mile (12,874.8-km) round trip to play at Lille in the French Cup in January 2024, only to lose 12–0.

VETERAN CYCLIST ↗ At age 90, Peter Langford cycled the length of the UK—1,100 miles (1,770.3 km) from Land's End, Cornwall, to John O'Groats, Scotland—in only 30 days. He had cycled the route three times before, at ages 75, 80, and 85.

Music on Wheels

Chloe Marie Aston from Devon, England, has a very special bike—with a piano attached to it! She loves performing and wanted to share music in a fun way. In 2019, her dad helped turn an offbeat idea into reality. And so the Piano Bike was born! Chloe has since pedaled and played the wheeled instrument in more than 200 towns across the UK.

SOLO EFFORT ↗ Swedish basketball player Mats Wermelin once scored 272 points in a game. And he was only 13 at the time! It happened at a tournament in Stockholm in 1974. Young Mats scored every point in his team's 272–0 win.

ORGAN PLAYER

Nancy Faust was the organist for the Chicago White Sox baseball team for 41 years. She performed at games from 1970 to 2010. During that time, she missed only seven scheduled appearances—for funerals and when she gave birth to her son.

HALLOWEEN RIDE ↗ For Halloween, cyclist Rebecca Laurel mapped out the shape of a skeleton on her GPS device. She did it by riding 69 miles (111 km) around Leicester, England, for more than six hours. She had previously ridden routes in the shape of a pumpkin, a ghost, and a witch.

ROLL RUN ↗ Bradley Whalen-Griffiths completed a marathon on the streets of Newcastle upon Tyne, England. Along his way he stopped at all 29 locations of local chain Greggs Bakery. And at each shop he ate a sausage roll! It took him 5 1/2 hours to run the 26.2 miles (41.8 km), and he consumed 9,600 calories.

VOCAL VISION

Romanie-Jade Tulloch from Nottingham, England, turns her face into a stage for stars!

Painting a mouth on her eye!

Also known as RJ, the makeup artist paints celebs like Beyoncé and Sabrina Carpenter on her face. Her trick is to use her eye as the celeb's mouth. When she blinks, it looks like the star is singing! She only uses regular makeup, never paint. Some designs can take up to 16 hours to finish! She also creates stunning surreal makeup illusions. RJ's fun and wild designs show that makeup isn't just for style—it can also make amazing art!

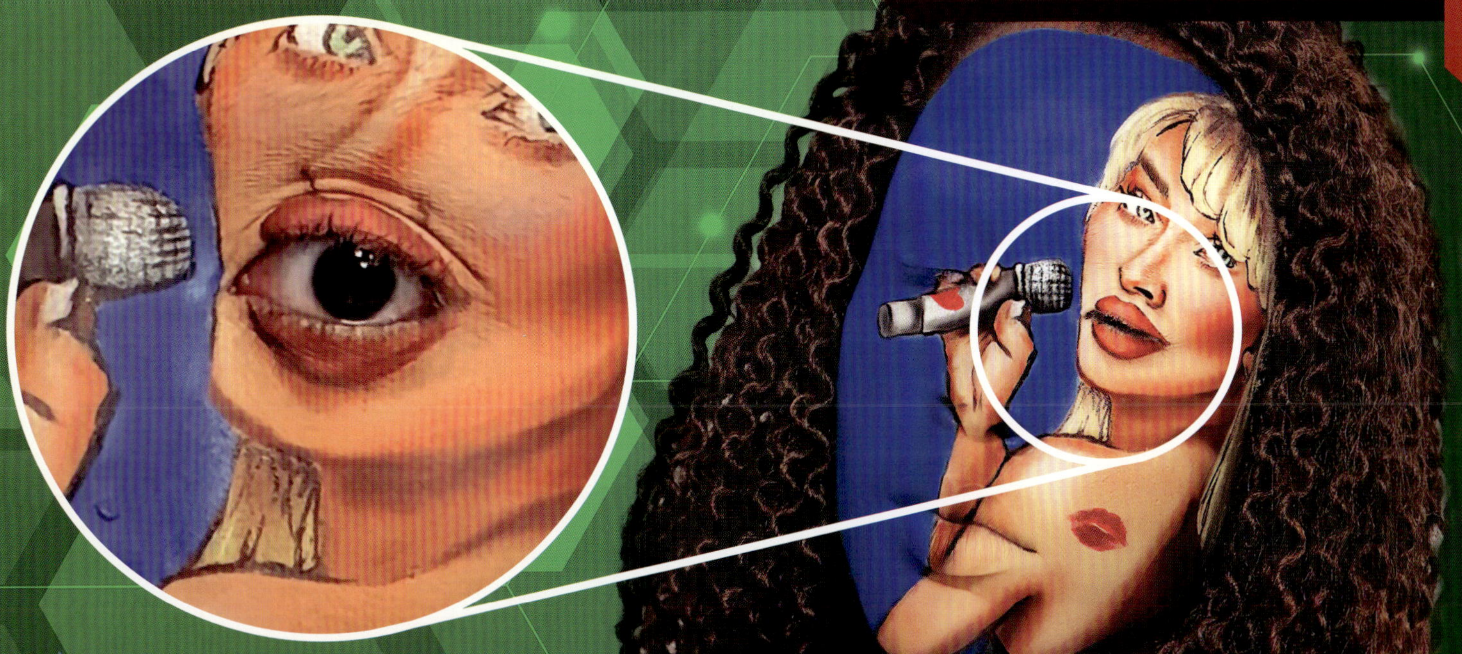

Romanie-Jade's eye becomes the celebrity's mouth!

Home Sweet Hive

Beekeepers in Slovenia paint their hives with detailed works of art! It is a tradition that dates back hundreds of years. The art might show stories from the Bible, old legends, or scenes of daily life. It was once thought that the panels were painted so bees would recognize their own hives! Some believed the art would ward off bad luck and keep the bees safe. When a hive is no longer used, the art might be sold. The panels have become popular souvenirs for tourists. Beekeeping is an important part of the country's culture—about one out of every 200 people in Slovenia keeps bees!

BEE CREATIVE!

PROLIFIC POET U.S. poet Emily Dickinson wrote almost 1,800 poems—but only 10 were published during her lifetime.

GRADE CHANGE The Beach Boys' Brian Wilson was writing songs while still in school. He submitted the band's debut single "Surfin'" to his music teacher at Hawthorne High School in California. The teacher was not impressed and gave Wilson an F for it. In 2018, nearly 60 years later, the school retrospectively changed his grade to an A.

BLOOD DRINK Eighteenth-century French writer Voltaire once drank blood from a bull on his country estate. He did it to disprove the ancient Greek theory that bull's blood was poisonous.

PUMPKIN MOSAIC Ian Nelson created a huge mosaic on his farm in Hampshire, England. Using 10,000 pumpkins and squashes, he recreated Michael Keaton's character in the 2024 film *Beetlejuice Beetlejuice*.

BAD POET Whenever he performed in public, nineteenth-century Scottish poet William McGonagall carried an umbrella with him. He was famous for being a bad poet, so angry audiences would pelt him with eggs, flour, vegetables, and rotten fruit. The umbrella protected him a little!

STRANGE DREAM The Jimi Hendrix song "Purple Haze" was inspired by a dream he had where he could walk underwater.

DYLAN CLASSIC Bob Dylan has spent nearly nine days of his life singing "Like a Rolling Stone." The song is six minutes long, and he has played it live more than 2,000 times.

SMILEY FACES Japanese ballpoint pen artist Asuka Sato once spent six days drawing 29,249 smiley faces on postcards. She only stopped when her pen ran out.

QUICK CHANGE In just one show, 17-year-old English actor Des Coghlan-Forbes had 37 costume changes. He starred in the National Youth Music Theatre's 2024 production of the musical *Our House* in London. Some of his changes were carried out in less than five seconds.

HEAVENLY STAR Actress Nicole Kidman was born in Honolulu. She was given the Hawaiian name Hokulani, meaning "heavenly star."

SIDE JOBS Even after he became famous, musician Philip Glass continued to support himself by working as a plumber and a cabbie in New York.

Melting POINT!

Swiss artist Urs Fischer makes wax sculptures that double as giant candles!

His wax figures are usually shaped like people. And they're built to burn! He and his team use scans and 3D printing to mold the wax into detailed shapes. Each piece contains multiple wicks so the wax melts evenly. As the flames burn, the sculptures drip, sag, and twist into weird new shapes, before melting into puddles of wax. Each piece varies in how long it can last due to size and how many wicks are lit.

Urs Fischer's self-portrait in wax.

BURNING THE CANDLE AT BOTH ENDS!

BEAD by BEAD

Galissa Golovan of Glazov, Russia, creates detailed handbags using thousands of beads, and she sews each one on by hand!

The custom-shaped bags range from creepy crawlers to iconic film characters. Galissa's bead art started off as just flat portraits. Then she decided to challenge herself and began making bags as well. She loves to show facial expressions. Just look at how she captured the main character of the film *Mrs. Doubtfire*! She draws inspiration from film, music, and art. Each eye-catching bag takes many hours to complete. She spent more than 80 hours just on a spider! She improvises on each piece, as she never knows which beads she will use.

Iconic scene from Mrs. Doubtfire made with beads!

Incredible detail!

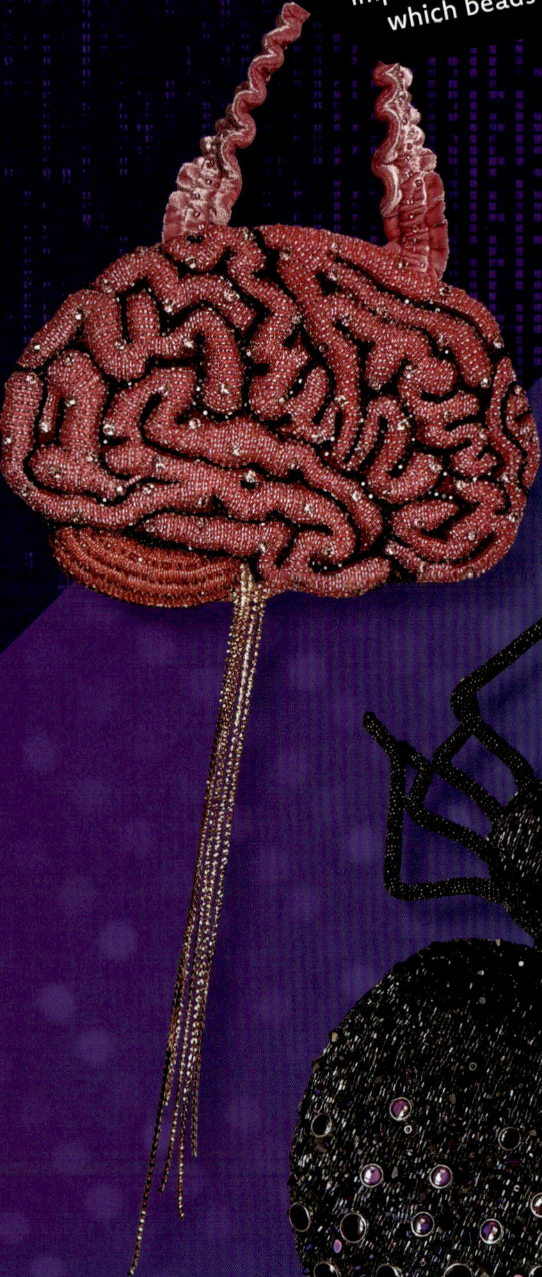

MAGNIFICENT MEMORY ↗ Over a period of nine years, from 1993 to 2001, American actor John Basinger memorized more than 60,000 words of John Milton's epic seventeenth-century poem *Paradise Lost*. He spent 3,000 hours learning the text, which runs to 12 books, by reciting it out loud, line by line, for an hour a day. When he had finished, he performed it in a live recital that lasted three days.

FORTUNATE FIND ↗ A bottle-shaped glass vase purchased for $3.99 by Jessica Vincent at a Goodwill store in Hanover County, Virginia, turned out to be a rare piece by Italian artist Carlo Scarpa. Six months later it sold for around $107,000.

BACK TO LIFE ↗ Bujji Aamma woke up in a hearse moments before she was due to be cremated. She was thought to have died following a fire in her home, and a few days later, her husband arranged for her to be transported to the cremation ground in a hearse.

KARATE KID

U.S. actor Taylor Lautner, who played werewolf Jacob Black in *The Twilight Saga* film series, was a Junior World Champion of karate. He began doing martial arts when he was six and became a black belt at 10. By the time he finished at 14, he was a four-time Junior World Champion.

CHILLED OUT ↗ U.S. novelist Truman Capote often wrote lying down, either in bed or on a couch, and described himself as a "completely horizontal author." He claimed it helped him think.

AVATAR FAN ↗ Jessica Carey of Oklahoma has more than 2,000 items of memorabilia relating to the *Avatar: The Last Airbender* franchise, including a pilot script, which she bought on eBay.

BOTTLE TREE ↗ To raise environmental awareness, sculptor Robert Marshall constructed a tree that is around 25 feet (7.6 m) tall from the 700 plastic bottles that his family had used over the past year.

MOVIE MORTALITY ↗ British actor Christopher Lee, who starred in many horror movies as well as the *Star Wars* and *The Lord of the Rings* franchises, died on screen 70 times. That's more than a quarter of the films in which he was featured!

RIPLEY'S COLLECTION

EXHIBIT NO. 175843

Movie Magic

This is a cast of actor Robin Williams's face. It was made from molds used to create his character's disguise in the 1993 film *Mrs. Doubtfire*. It took the makeup team more than four hours each day to transform Robin Williams into the iconic British nanny.

OSCAR-WINNING MAKEUP!

Actor Robin Williams as Mrs. Doubtfire (above) and as he normally appeared (right).

SEE MORE!

POP CULTURE

Dough Dreams

Have you ever tried to bake cookie dough in a shape, only for it to become a blob in the oven? The Flower Cookies Lady doesn't have that problem!

Based in Buenos Aires, Argentina, she bakes 3D cookies with amazing detail. She first tried sculpting cookie dough when her power went out one day. She had already made the dough but couldn't bake it, so she molded it into flowers instead! That's how she became known as the Flower Cookies Lady. She then spent a year perfecting her dough recipe so it holds its shape better. She now sculpts not just flowers, but also animals, characters, and even entire scenes!

This biblically accurate angel cookie took 10 hours to make!

HALF-MILE SHOELACE ↗ A shoelace more than half a mile long was created in St. Louis, Missouri, in 2024. The City Museum teamed up with The Shoelace Factory to create the 2,729.3-foot-long (831.9-m) shoelace. It took around 24 hours to weave the lace on one of the factory's antique textile machines that dates back to 1890.

FAMILY TREE ↗ For 103 years, Dorothy Grant's family kept a 2.5-foot-tall (0.8-m) artificial Christmas tree that her mother had purchased in London, England, in 1920. Grant died in 2014, and nine years later the tree was sold for more than $4,000—over 56,000 times its original price.

PUZZLES APLENTY ↗ Since 2019, husband and wife John and Kyle Walczak have built a collection of more than 2,000 jigsaw puzzles. Their biggest is a 60,000-piece map of the world that took them 10 months to complete.

SAHARA STORM ↗ When a sandstorm during the 1994 Marathon des Sables caused him to be lost in the Sahara for nine days, Italian runner Mauro Prosperi stayed alive by drinking his own urine and the blood of bats. He had veered over 180 miles (289.7 km) off course in temperatures that can exceed 120°F (48.9°C). Despite having to eat raw snakes and lizards to survive, he went on to complete the race a few years later.

HOME RUNS ↗ Baseball-playing brothers Justin and B. J. Upton hit their 100th career home runs on the same day. On August 3, 2012, Justin hit a home run for the Arizona Diamondbacks against the Philadelphia Phillies. Less than an hour later, B. J. did the same for the Tampa Bay Rays against the Baltimore Orioles. The brothers had also hit their 99th home runs on the same day, two weeks earlier, on July 20.

BIG BAGUETTE ↗ Bakers in Paris, France, made a 461-foot-long (140.5-m) baguette—nearly six times the length of a tennis court. It was about 235 times longer than a standard baguette and was cooked in a specially built, slow-moving oven on wheels.

Wayne Wright, artist

Spilled Milk

Artist Wayne Wright of Shirley, England, doesn't cry over spilled milk—he turns it into works of art! He captures images of famous people and characters. Sometimes Wayne uses coffee for his liquid portraits. He also tried tea and gravy, but those did not turn out so great! To make his art, he pours a splash of milk or coffee onto a surface and then gently moves it into place with his hands or a paintbrush. While Wayne can keep art made with coffee, the milk art is temporary and gets wiped away once completed!

Keanu Reeves

Brad Pitt

Prince

Eminem

Yabba Dabba Dome!

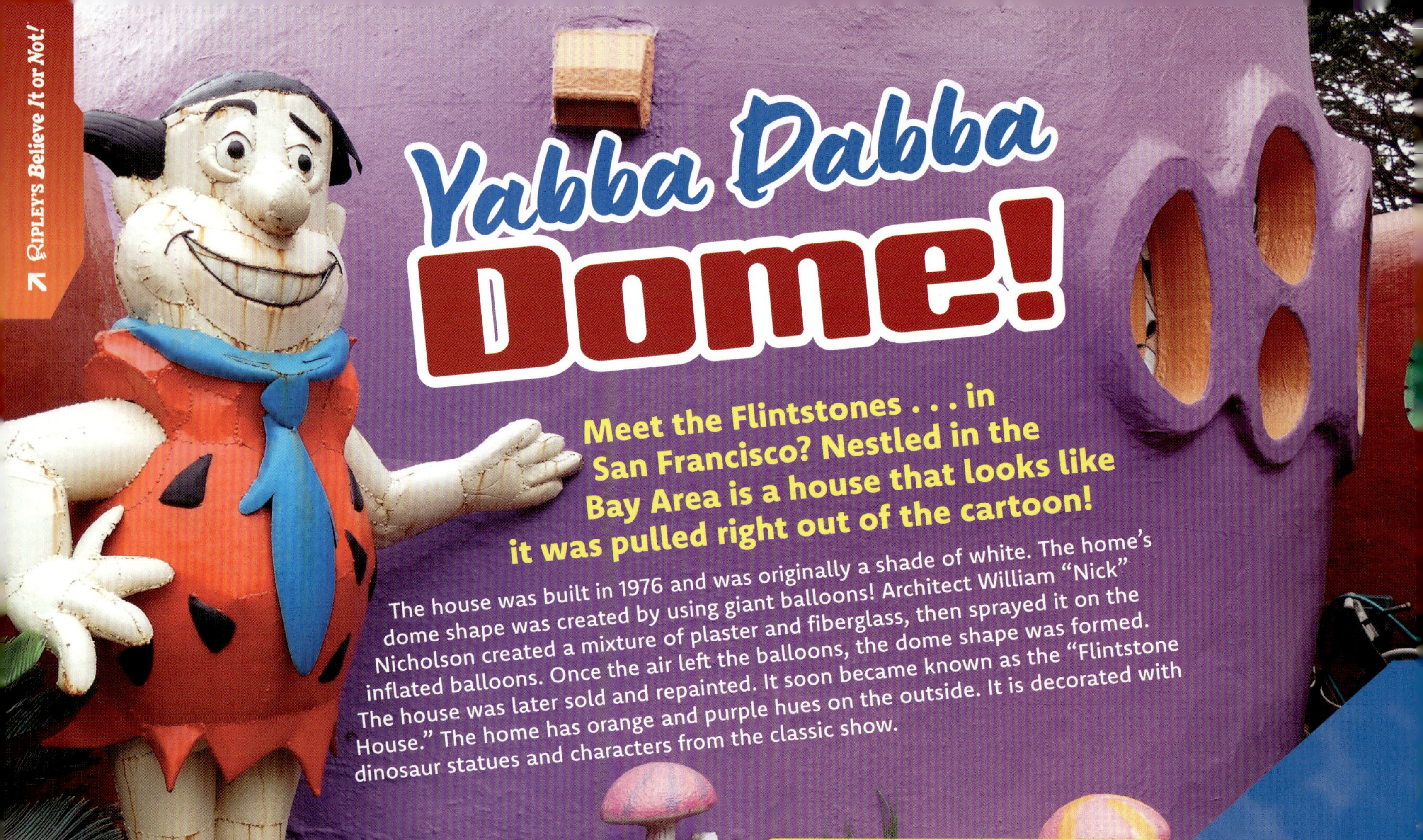

Meet the Flintstones . . . in San Francisco? Nestled in the Bay Area is a house that looks like it was pulled right out of the cartoon!

The house was built in 1976 and was originally a shade of white. The home's dome shape was created by using giant balloons! Architect William "Nick" Nicholson created a mixture of plaster and fiberglass, then sprayed it on the inflated balloons. Once the air left the balloons, the dome shape was formed. The house was later sold and repainted. It soon became known as the "Flintstone House." The home has orange and purple hues on the outside. It is decorated with dinosaur statues and characters from the classic show.

BUILT WITH GIANT BALLOONS!

FAN REWARD ↗ *Star Wars* fan James Jorgensen, of Massachusetts, won a $5.37 million lottery jackpot on *Star Wars* Day—May 4.

DRY ICE ↗ Over the course of 15 years between its 2003 premiere and 2018, the Broadway run of the musical *Wicked* used more than 470 tons of dry ice.

ONE-WAY WRITING ↗ Twentieth-century U.S. author Damon Runyon almost always avoided using the past tense in his writing.

DARTH DISAPPEARANCE ↗ Darth Vader only appeared on screen for 8 minutes and 6 seconds in the original *Star Wars* movie—just 6 percent of the entire film.

BIRD BREAK ↗ During the 1916 Easter Rising, which lasted six days, gunfire exchanges between British and Irish forces around Saint Stephen's Green in Dublin were halted every day to allow park-keeper James Kearney to feed the ducks.

RARE BILL ↗ A rare 1934 $10,000 bill from the era of the Great Depression sold at auction in 2023 for $480,000.

HOT DOGS ↗ Around 20 million hot dogs are eaten by baseball fans during an MLB season.

WALKING TOUR

Folk music duo Filkin's Drift, a.k.a. Chris Roberts and Seth Bye, walked 870 miles (1,400.1 km) around Wales with their instruments (a guitar and a fiddle) strapped to their backs. They played 50 gigs on their 59-day walking tour.

Seeing Double

This painting isn't the *Mona Lisa*—it's a copy! The Prado Museum in Madrid, Spain, restored the work of art. It shows new incredible details. We can now see the young woman's eyebrows! Also, check out the curly texture in her hair. There is even more detail in the background! It shows a rocky landscape in two different seasons.

No one knows who painted it. However, it was likely made by one of Leonardo da Vinci's students around the same time as the original.

Original

Star-Crossed Truckers

A production of Shakespeare's *Romeo and Juliet* in Estonia had an unusual cast—cars, trucks, and more! The play was set in a quarry. The stars of the show were a rally truck for Romeo and a pickup truck for Juliet. Drivers moved the trucks to make them act like they were in love. Sometimes they even "kissed!" While the concept seems silly, the play's drama wasn't forgotten. Two excavators used their arms to recreate the deadly duel between Tybalt and Mercutio.

MELON DEAL ↗ French author Alexandre Dumas had a taste for melons. In 1864, the author of *The Count of Monte Cristo* and *The Three Musketeers* donated more than 300 copies of his published books to a library in Cavaillon. In return, he asked for 12 melons a year for the rest of his life. So the town sent him a dozen melons every summer until his death in 1870.

BOXING CATS ↗ An 1894 short film by Thomas Edison was a precursor to today's online cat videos. Filmed at Edison's New York studio, it was titled *Professor Welton's Boxing Cats.* It showed two cats wearing gloves in a boxing ring. The boxers were the star attraction of Henry Welton's cat circus, which also featured cats riding bicycles.

FIRE EATER ↗ Before becoming James Bond, Irish actor Pierce Brosnan was a professional fire eater in his teens. He finally gave it up after burning his mouth on a 1997 edition of the TV show *Muppets Tonight.*

YOUNG DRUMMER

At only three years old, U.S. actor and musician Richard Keith earned $500 a week as a professional drummer. That was in the 1950s—so it works out to more than $5,000 in today's money. Keith, who played Little Ricky in the TV show *I Love Lucy*, played the drums with music ensemble Horace Heidt and His Orchestra.

MUSICAL TOOTHBRUSH ↗ U.S. band Green Day marked the 30th anniversary of their album *Dookie* by reissuing tracks from it on 15 unusual devices. These included an electric toothbrush, a doorbell, an answering machine, and an animatronic singing fish.

OWL HUNT ↗ For 31 years, more than 200,000 people searched for an owl statue that was buried somewhere in France. The owl was made from gold, silver, and diamonds. The quest to find it was based on a 1993 book, *On the Trail of the Golden Owl*, by Régis Hauser and Michel Becker. They had buried the $165,000 statue in a secret place. To locate it, participants first had to solve 11 puzzles from the book. Then they had to find and solve a hidden 12th puzzle. The owl was finally found in 2024.

2,000+ STRIKES ↗ A four-man team from Kentucky—Steve Wiseman, Trace Wiseman, Kyle Reed, and Erik Howard—bowled 2,032 strikes in 24 hours at Kingpin Lanes in Jeffersontown.

Apartment of Dreams

Sarah Boll turned her New York City apartment into the *Titanic*!

As soon as you opened the door, it looked like you were stepping onto the iconic ship. Portholes on the wall gave the illusion that the sea is just steps away. One bedroom even looked like the iceberg just hit. Sarah draped fabric from the ceiling to give off an icy vibe. She also gave the floor its own special treatment—blue carpet with a shiny overlay to mimic the ocean's surface. Her design was inspired by both the real ship and the movie. Sarah spent more than a year living inside her ocean-themed creation. After that, she changed things up and transformed it into the magical Land of Oz!

SARAH SINKS INTO HER ICY SHIP!

HOUSE OF WAX

Prop maker Rob Cametti turned his Florida home into a monster museum!

Each October, he calls it the "MuckleBones Monster Museum." It's full of all things spooky and strange! He has skeletons, aliens, and clowns. Some classic movie monsters are lurking, too. Watch out for Frankenstein's creature! Rob has more than 60 full-size figures in his collection, plus a couple hundred busts. He even got one wax head from Ripley's Believe It or Not! He builds many monsters himself and stores extra in a warehouse. Around 600 people visit each year, and he donates any money he makes to charity.

ENTER IF YOU DARE!

Rob Cametti and his family

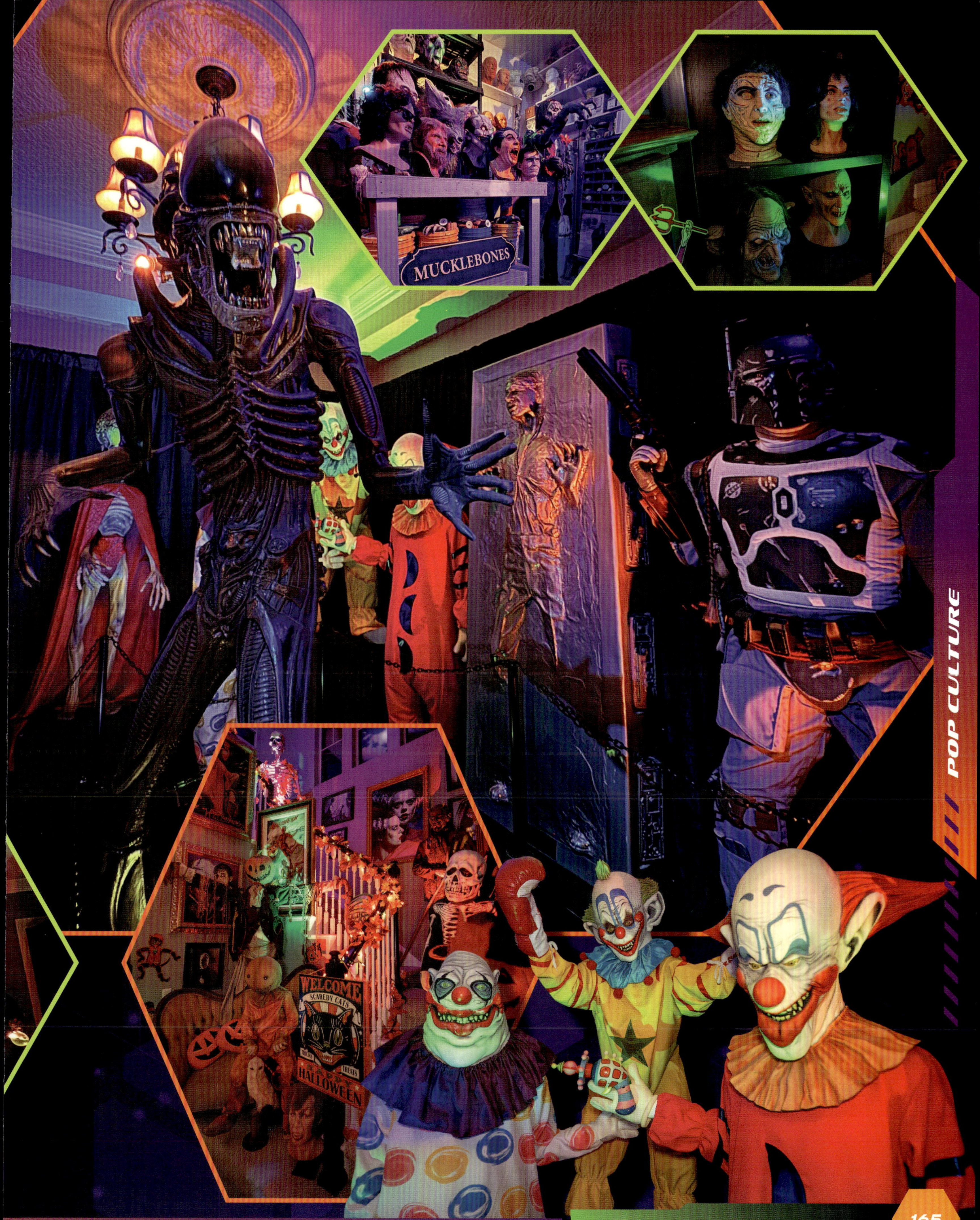
MUCKLEBONES
WELCOME
SCAREDY CATS
HALLOWEEN

Condiment KING

RIPLEY'S EXCLUSIVE

Eric Thompson of Helotes, Texas, has a passion that's truly one of a kind—he collects empty sauce packets!

From ketchup to soy sauce, he saves, cleans, and displays them like tiny works of art. He began collecting in 2007 while in college, inspired by how the sauces in the campus dining hall were arranged by color. Eric now has thousands of packets! He empties and cleans each one, then stores them in baseball card sleeves. Ripley's reached out to Eric to learn more about his collection.

" It keeps me up at night. I need one!

Q: What is your favorite packet?

A: I was born and raised in Pennsylvania, so I have a deep affinity for Heinz packets. When I think of a "condiment packet," my mind immediately goes to that classic Heinz ketchup packet with the bottle of Heinz ketchup on the front.

Q: What is the rarest or most interesting packet you own?

A: In the collection, there is only one single Worcestershire sauce packet. The fact that I've never seen another one makes it a unique anomaly.

Q: Is there a "holy grail" you're still searching for?

A: Some Kmart stores had branded ketchup packets with the Kmart logo on them. There are very few images of this—but enough to know that it existed. It keeps me up at night. I need one!

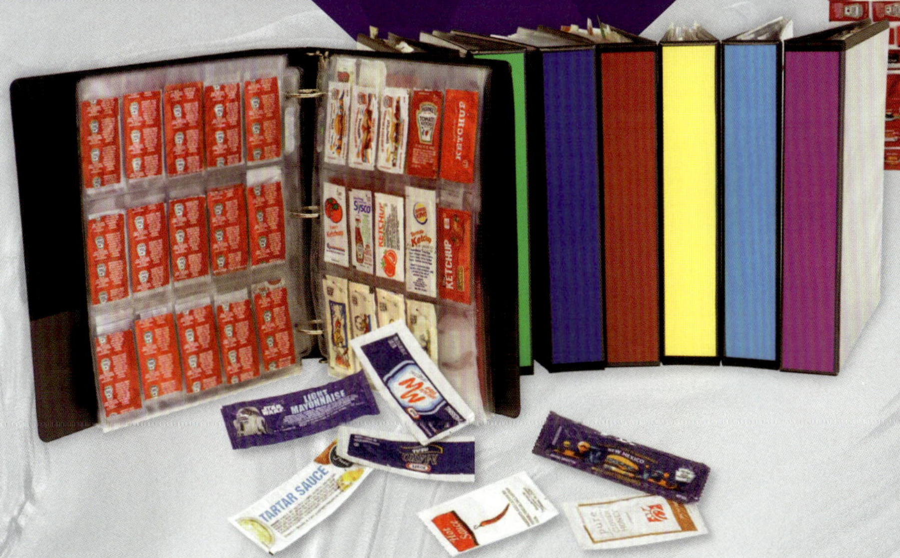

Q: What's the oldest packet in the collection?

A: I have several vintage packets, the oldest of which is likely from the very late 1960s. A company called Serv-A-Portion made packets with two instructions—"hold here" and "tear here"—a good indication that the packet is from the dawn of the invention.

Q: How do you decide which ones are worth keeping?

A: If the packet is unique and not represented in the collection, it's an obvious keeper. I consider packet redesigns to be new entries as well, as part of the collection idea is to track changes over time.

Q: What are your plans for the collection?

A: My ultimate goal will be to donate the collection to the Smithsonian. I think there's merit in the Americana factor of it. Until then, I'll keep collecting and documenting the collection for everyone to enjoy.

EXHIBIT NO. 176319

A New Rope

Florida artist Mateo Blanco created a larger-than-life sculpture of Princess Leia out of rope! He made it in layers. The spaces between the layers make it so you have to view the piece from the right angle to really see the Star Wars character with her iconic buns.

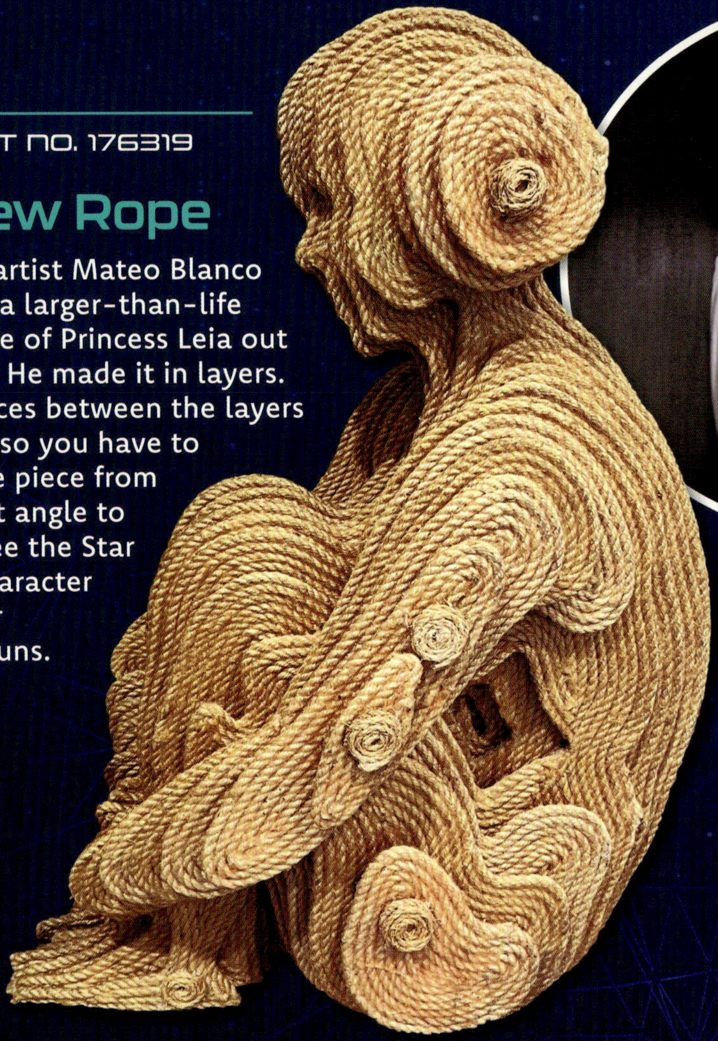

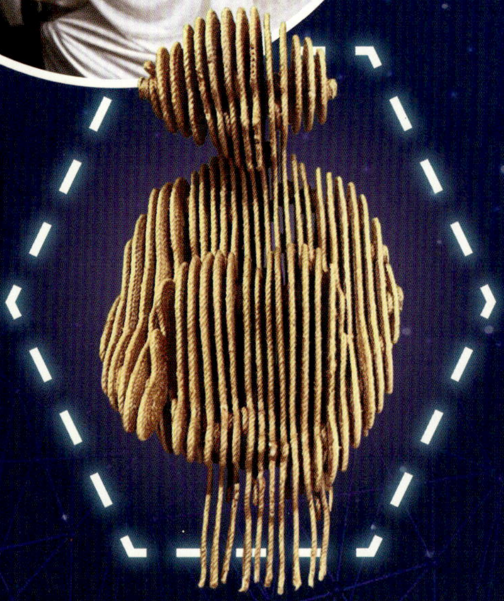

Front view

SEE MORE!

EXHIBIT NO. 176290 & 176291

Cowabunga Crew

These Teenage Mutant Ninja Turtles heads come straight from the 1990s! They were real movie props used for the characters of Donatello and Michaelangelo. The heads were made from latex and filled with foam. Their detailed faces helped bring the famous turtles to life on the big screen.

EXHIBIT NO. 176289

Rolling Rescue

A real-life Tonka truck is rolling through town! This drivable fire truck is built to look just like the trucks from the toy children's book *Trucks around Town* by Thomas LaPadula. It's fully loaded with flashing lights, a siren, and a working hose reel. It even has a cute Dalmatian dog in the back!

UP NEXT...

AROUND THE WORLD

FOOD FIGHT

At the yearly Gran Tomatina festival in Sutamarchán, Colombia, people throw tomatoes just for fun!

In 2025, more than 20,000 people joined the food fight. Around 22,000 pounds (9,979 kg) of squishy tomatoes too ripe to sell or eat were thrown! People wore old clothes, laughed, and got covered in red juice! The festival lasts three days and also includes games, music, and parades. The event is inspired by Spain's famous La Tomatina festival. It started in 2004 to celebrate local tomato farmers, and now it's one of the biggest—and messiest—parties in the country.

Baby Bread

It is common for holidays to be paired with certain foods. In parts of South America, many celebrate All Saints' Day and All Souls' Day with t'anta wawa—baby bread! Families bring this baked good with them while visiting deceased loved ones at the cemetery. T'anta wawa is shaped like a baby wrapped in a blanket, with only a doll's head peeking out. For some, it represents the loss of a child. For others, the baby bread is a symbol of life!

Onion Island

Awaji Island in Japan grows some of the sweetest onions in the world. During the spring harvest, the area smells like onions every day! They grow so well there because of the island's rich soil and sunny weather. Local restaurants serve things like onion burgers and steamed onions with butter. There's even a giant onion statue to honor their prized crop!

Snow GLOW

When snow falls on Hailin City, a.k.a. China's Snow Town, it turns into a real-life winter wonderland!

Tucked away in the mountains of Heilongjiang Province, snow can reach up to 6 feet (1.8 m) deep every year. In winter, the snow is so thick and fluffy that it almost doesn't look real. The town's dreamy appearance makes it a popular place to film movies and TV shows. Tourists come from all over to walk through glowing lantern streets, try winter sports, and see the snow sparkle under the lights. It's pure snowy magic!

Faster Pastures

In Thailand, some farmers have turned their farming tractors into racing machines! These colorful tractors race on dirt tracks in rice fields. The racers stand up to drive them and wear helmets for safety. The tracks are bumpy and muddy, making it extra exciting for racers—and the fans watching from the sidelines! Some farmers build low-to-the-ground versions that look more like small cars with steering wheels and brakes.

FARMERS, START YOUR ENGINES!

SILLY SPECTACLE ↗ The Saint Stupid's Day Parade takes place each year in San Francisco on April 1. A celebration of absurdity, it was founded in 1979 by Ed Holmes (a.k.a. Bishop Joey from the Church of the Last Laugh) and involves music, colorful costumes, and an exchange of socks outside the historic Stock Exchange Tower.

AVOCADO ALP ↗ For the Cinco de Mayo celebration on May 5, 2024, El Rio Grande Latin Market in Dallas, Texas, built a display with 301,000 avocados.

FULL FAMILY ↗ In November 2023, 199 members of the same family were living in a building in Baktawng, India. They are the family of the late Pu Zionnghaka, who built the house and had 38 wives.

FOREVER FIRE

A fire inside a temple in Yazd, Iran, has burned continuously for more than 1,550 years. The fire has been allowed to burn since 470 AD and is kept alight by a person called a Hirob, who adds dry wood several times a day.

LOCAL LANDMARK ↗ A church in Rosslyn, Virginia, is located directly above a gas station. The Arlington Temple United Methodist Church is known locally as "Our Lady of Exxon" in reference to its association with the gas station since 1971.

LOW LOGS ↗ The Italian city of Venice was built on a foundation of millions of underwater logs. Wooden platforms were built on top of the logs; then buildings were constructed on the platforms.

DARK SHOP ↗ For more than 25 years, the Los Angeles coroner's office had its own gift shop, known as Skeletons in the Closet, where visitors could buy body bags, plastic skeletons, death-themed shirts, and beach towels bearing images of a chalk body outline.

RIVER RUMBLE

Every summer in Bath, Illinois, brave teams take to the river to battle fish that fly!

At the Redneck Fishing Tournament, Asian carp leap from the river like rockets. When boats speed by, the carp jump high—sometimes right into people's faces! Teams wear helmets and carry nets, trying to catch the fish in midair. No fishing poles are allowed during the contest. The goal is to catch as many carp as possible, since the fish are an invasive species. Previous winners have caught hundreds of fish in just two hours!

Steep Street

Canton Avenue in Pittsburgh, Pennsylvania, is one of the steepest streets in the world! For every 100 feet (30.5 m) you climb, you get 37 feet (11.3 m) higher. It's the perfect place for a grueling uphill challenge! Every October, cyclists take part in a race around the steepest climbs of Pittsburgh, including Canton Avenue. The cyclists must make it from the bottom to the top of each hill in the fastest time—hopefully without falling off!

Ship Ahoy!

Johan Helberg, from Norway, stayed sound asleep when a 443-foot (135-m) container ship ran aground—right into his front yard! Johan's house is near the water's edge. The front of the ship parked right next to his house, missing the building by just a few feet. Johan only realized what had happened when a neighbor repeatedly rang his doorbell to check if he was okay, which woke him up.

Antler Antics

Each fall, the villagers of Abbots Bromley in England perform a "horn dance" while carrying giant antlers! Six dancers dress as deer and hold a set of antlers. The heaviest weighs more than 25 pounds (11.3 kg)! Other characters include a fool, hobby horse, bowman, and Maid Marian. The performers travel for around 10 miles (16.1 km), stopping many times to perform the horn dance. The tradition is more than 800 years old and is thought to bring luck while hunting.

BATMAN'S CITY The Australian city of Melbourne was once called Batmania. It was named after explorer John Batman, who founded a settlement there in 1835.

EXCLAMATION POINTS There are two towns in the world with an exclamation point in their official name. They are Westward Ho! in Devon, England, and Saint-Louis-du-Ha!-Ha! in Quebec, Canada.

VAST AIRPORT Denver International Airport in Colorado covers an area of 53 square miles (137.3 sq km). It is more than double the size of Manhattan and larger than the city boundaries of San Francisco and Boston.

CANDY DESK A desk in the U.S. Senate has a drawer full of candy. It is a tradition that started in 1965. Whichever senator sits at the desk fills the drawer with candy from their home state for colleagues to eat.

Sheepish Stones

On Estonia's Saaremaa Island, you can visit a park full of stone sheep, just for fun! It was thought up by a local politician, Mart Maastik. There are around 300 statues to meet, some in the "lamb parliament" and some in the "lamb army." The army is overseen by stone generals Moose and Bear! There's even a sheep dance festival. It's a wacky world where sheep rule the land—stone-faced!

HOMECOMING *Herd*

PARTY UNTIL THE COWS COME HOME!

Farmers near the Alps mountain range put on homecoming parties for their cows!

Every summer, cows are taken up into the mountains to graze. When fall arrives, it's time for them to come home. And it's time to party! Thousands of people enjoy these celebrations throughout the region. There's music, food, and dancing, too. The cows wear beautiful flower headdresses and giant bells as they walk through the villages. The procession is known as an Almabtrieb. It's a way to give thanks for the safe return of the cattle!

CLOUD

The sky is the limit—literally—on China's Huajiang Grand Canyon Bridge!

The bridge sits about 2,050 feet (624.8 m) above the Beipan River. The river winds its way through a deep gorge. To stretch across it, the bridge needed to be 4,600 feet (1,402.1 m) long. The project took close to four years to complete. Before the bridge was finished, it took about two hours to drive from one side of the canyon to the other. Now it takes drivers just two minutes!

BURIED TEMPLE The Nageswara Swamy temple in Perumallapadu, India, was buried beneath sand for more than 80 years. Terrible floods in 1850 changed the course of the Penna River and redirected sand onto the temple. By 1940, it was completely covered. Then, in 2024, villagers dug away the sand to reveal the lost temple.

FIRE PRECAUTION When wildfires are raging, some trees "hold their breath" to avoid inhaling smoke. Plants breathe through their leaf pores. But during fires some pine trees deliberately close these pores. They only reopen them when conditions improve.

TIME ZONES

The North and South Poles have no time zones. The lines of longitude that decide time zones meet at the poles. So the poles are in all of the world's 24 different time zones at once.

IMPOSSIBLE CLIMB A motocross hill climb near Silves, Portugal, is almost impossible to finish. In more than two decades only a handful of competitors have successfully completed Subida Impossível. Riders must steer their bikes 360 feet (110 m) up a rocky hill, without their feet ever touching the ground. In places, the hill has an extremely steep 80 percent gradient.

DEFYING GRAVITY Vehicles on Electric Brae, a short stretch of road in South Ayrshire, Scotland, appear to roll uphill. But they're not really defying gravity. It's just an optical illusion created by the surrounding landscape.

CRUISE

For tourists who want a perfect picture, there's a glass platform with a view of the canyon 2,600 feet (792.5 m) above the river!

GETTING SPRAYED DOWN!

ONE TON RUN

During the Hakata Gion Yamakasa festival, teams of men race through a city while carrying a 1-ton float!

Held in Fukuoka, Japan, the event starts before dawn. Spectators line the 3.1-mile (5-km) course and throw water to keep the runners cool. The men wear traditional costumes to partake in the race. The elaborately decorated floats can reach 32.8 feet (10 m) high. Each float is carried by around 30 men, with spare runners in the back to take over when the others get tired. Some men sit on the float and tell runners when to stop. Even the strongest runners need a rest after just a few minutes!

三番山笠

Fountain FORTUNE

So many coins are tossed into Rome's Trevi Fountain that it has to be cleaned out twice a week!

Every year, millions of people visit Italy and throw coins into the famous fountain to make a wish. With so many coins collected, the fountain is cleaned twice a week! It takes a few hours to clear the coins. Workers use brooms to sweep the coins into a line. Then a huge vacuum sucks them up. About 1.4 million Euros are collected every year and donated to local charities. Even if your wish doesn't come true, your coins help others!

FACT FILES

According to legend, using your right hand to toss a coin over your left shoulder and into the Trevi Fountain will ensure you return to Rome someday.

MONEY TALK

In 2024, **a U.S. dime** missing its mint mark was sold at auction for **$506,250!**

The Wright Brothers flipped a coin to decide which of them would be the first to pilot their plane.

The ceilings and walls of **McGuire's Irish Pub in Pensacola, Florida,** are plastered with over **$1 million** worth of bills!

In Canada, there is a limit to how many coins you can use to pay in a **single transaction.**

One million U.S. dollars in $100 bills weighs about **22 pounds (10 kg)!**

At around **1,200 years old,** the British pound is the world's **oldest legal tender** still in use.

The **ancient Mayans and Aztecs** used quetzal **tail feathers** as a form of currency.

RIPLEY'S COLLECTION

EXHIBIT NO. 168300

Pocket Change

Wander Martich of Grand Rapids, Michigan, made a giant penny out of 84,000 regular pennies! Her idea for the sculpture came from a time when her young daughters offered to help pay for things with the change in their piggy bank. Wander worked 10 hours a day for three months to make the 8-foot-wide (2.4-m) coin.

SEE MORE!

84,000 PENNIES!

AROUND THE WORLD

Last One Standing

People in Namur, Belgium, don't just walk on stilts—they battle on them! The tradition of jousting on tall wooden stilts has been around for more than 600 years. Over 6,000 people attend the Festival of Wallonia every September. The highlight is the battle for the Golden Stilt. Two teams face off as they try to knock each other down. Once a stilt walker falls, they cannot get back on their stilts. The last person standing wins the Golden Stilt for a year.

Tree Cake

Baumkuchen is a traditional German cake baked over fire on a spit! To make it, the baker must pay close attention. They watch over the cake for 90 minutes as it slowly rotates in a special oven. Every so often, they carefully pour on new layers of cake batter, until it has up to 25 layers! The resulting shape earned the treat its name—"Baumkuchen" means "tree cake!"

HIGH HONORS

Every year, the people of Nepal honor the god of rain with a 60-foot-tall (18.3-m) chariot!

The chariot is built as part of a month-long festival. It is decorated with flowers and symbols. Then a statue of the rain god Rato Machhindranath is placed inside. People pull the chariot through the city streets using two large ropes. Musicians play traditional music alongside the procession. The festival takes place right before monsoon season. It is believed the god will then send rain for the crops.

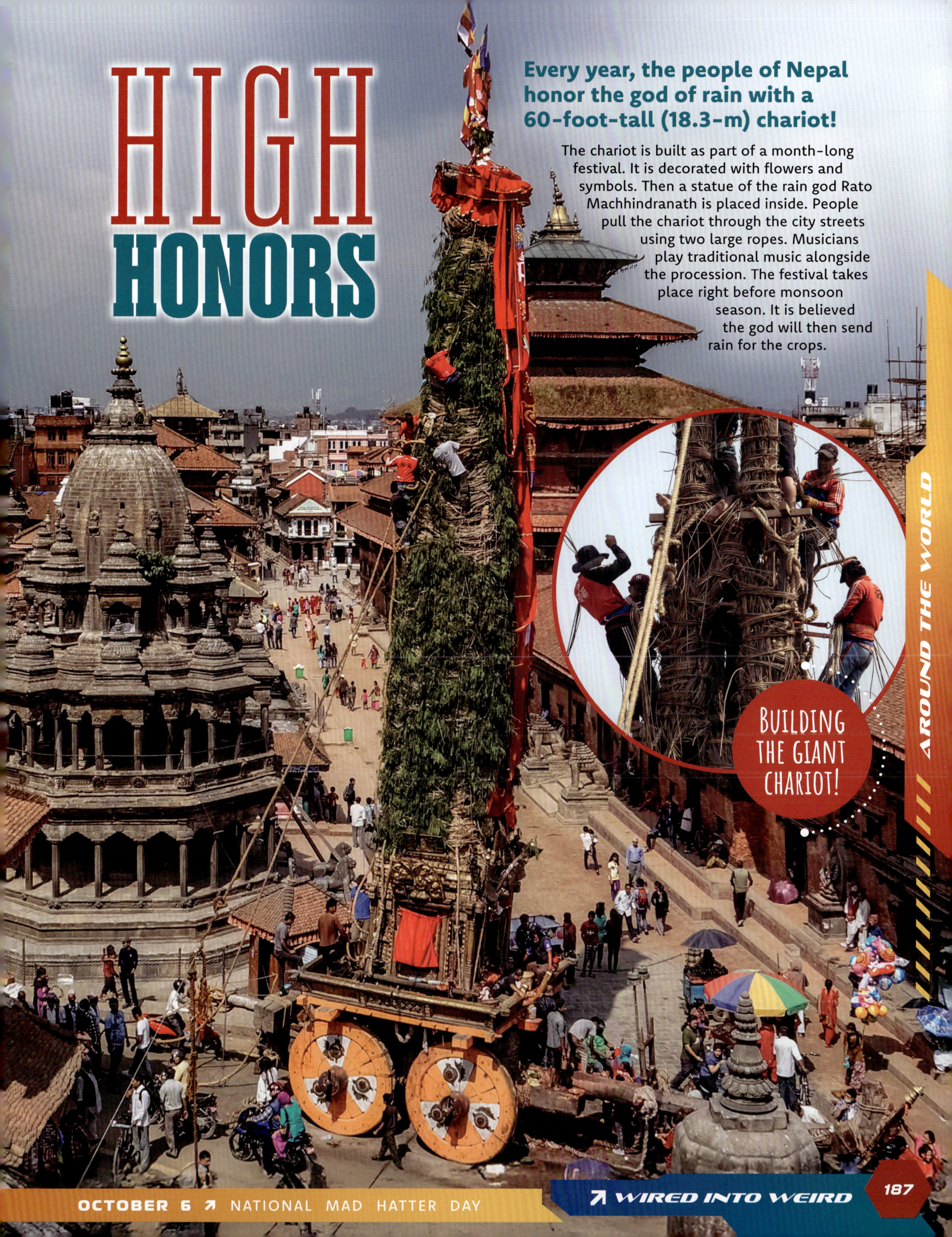

BUILDING THE GIANT CHARIOT!

MASKED Dancer

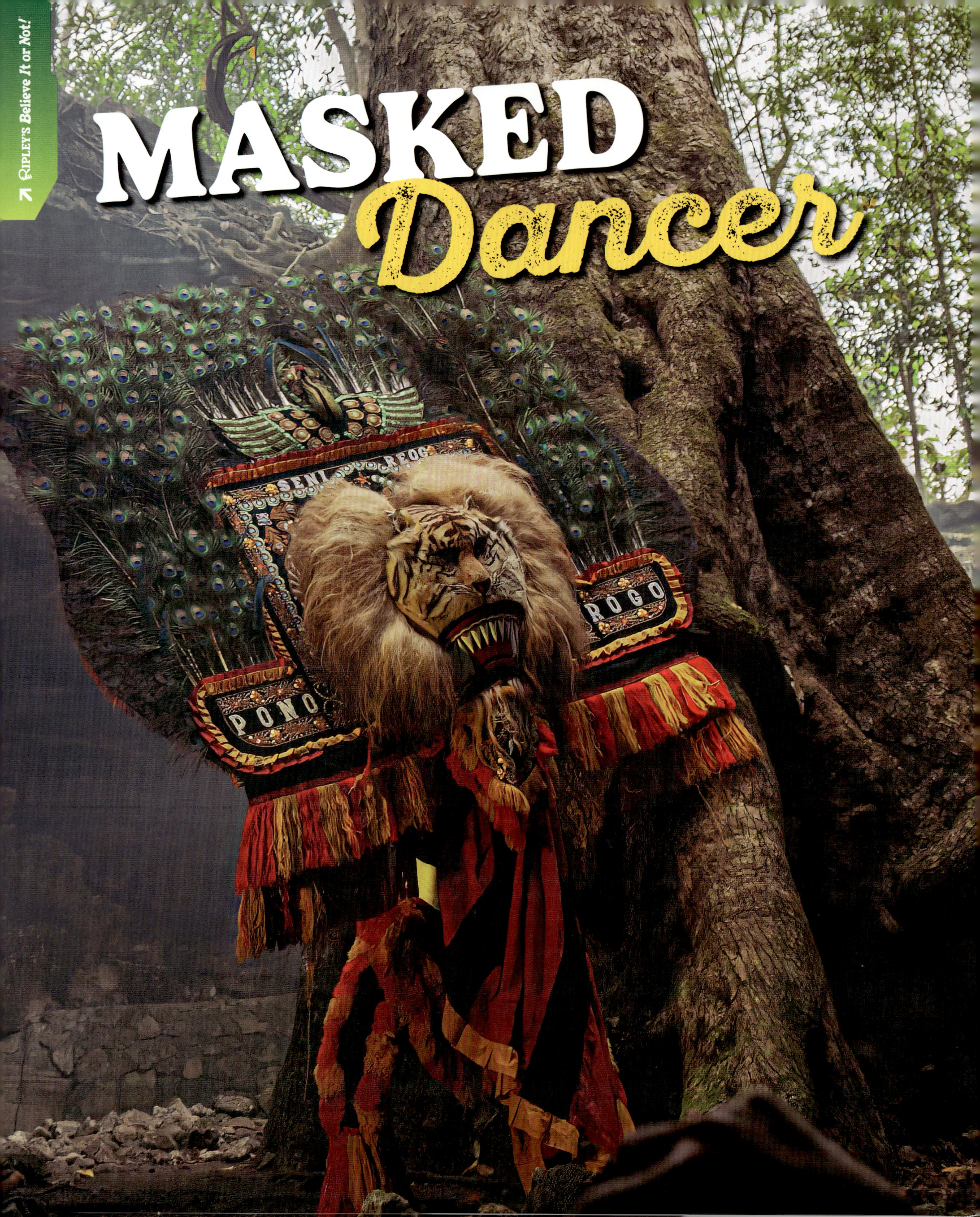

In Indonesia, there is a traditional dance in which a dancer wears a mask that weighs up to 110 pounds (49.9 kg) and carries it all with just their teeth!

It's called Reog Ponorogo, and it is performed at special events and celebrations. It even has its own festival! The masked dancer bites down on a hidden wooden bar to carry the large display. Sometimes a child will even sit on top of it while it's being worn! The mask is of a lion's face. It is surrounded by an array of peacock feathers. The tradition started in East Java, but there are many versions of the dance. It tells the story of a mythical battle between a king and the lion creature.

REOG PONOROGO DANCER FROM BEHIND

TOWN GIFT When wealthy Parisian Roger Thiberville died, he left over $10 million to the small French town of Thiberville—even though he had never been there. He did so simply because the town shares his last name.

POTHOLE PLANTATION A small banana plantation has sprung up in the middle of a busy street in Havana, Cuba. When a large pothole caused by a broken water pipe was not fully repaired, several banana plants took root there. Local residents water the trees daily so that they can enjoy the free fruit.

YELLOW SOIL The Texas city of Amarillo used to be called Oneida. Then nineteenth-century settlers observed the yellow soil that lined the banks of a nearby lake and creek. So they renamed it Amarillo, after the Spanish word for "yellow."

PLANE SUITE A hotel room in Amsterdam, the Netherlands, contains part of a real airplane! Inside the 737 Suite at the Corendon New-West Hotel, guests can explore the front section of an old Boeing 737 jet, including the cockpit and 13 seats. The plane's nose protrudes from the window. A recording of the captain's voice welcomes guests when they enter the room and turn on the lights.

LIBRARY COLLECTION The British Library in London, England, stores one copy of every book published in the UK and Ireland. In total, it houses more than 170 million artifacts, some dating back to 2000 BC. It has over 466 miles (750 km) of shelving, roughly the distance from London to Aberdeen, Scotland. If a visitor saw five items a day, it would take them more than 80,000 years to view the entire collection.

Stranger Praise

A middle-aged Japanese man known as "Uncle Praise" makes a living by praising total strangers in the street. In return for a small fee, he compliments around 30 people a day. He even has regular clients who call him when they need cheering up.

Pigeon Palaces

For hundreds of years, farmers in the Middle East built giant birdhouses that could house thousands of pigeons! Known as pigeon towers, they were made of mud bricks and covered with lime. The small entrance holes only allowed pigeons to enter. This kept out predators such as hawks! Inside, they looked like beehives with neat patterns of nesting ledges lining the walls. Some can still be seen today. Why did the farmers put in so much effort into towers for pigeons? Because their poop made great fertilizer for melon and cucumber crops!

FUTURISTIC FOREST

At the Gardens by the Bay in Singapore, more than 160,000 plants grow from the trunks of towering tech trees!

There are 18 of these "Supertrees," measuring around 82–165 feet (25–50.3 m) tall. They have thick trunks and winding branches, just like a tree in fall. They've been built to function in ways that are similar to real trees, too. They have solar panels to make their own energy. They collect rainwater to feed the plants growing on the trunks. And they even have a cooling system! The high-tech trees are home to plants like bromeliads, orchids, ferns, and tropical climbing flowers. And when darkness falls, the Supertrees put on a spectacular light show to draw in visitors at night, too!

An elevated walkway between two Supertrees offers a view of the Gardens from more than 72 feet (22 m) high!

1244
MARSHAL

RIDING IN VINTAGE STYLE!

AROUND THE WORLD

DAPPER DASH

Hundreds of people hop on their bikes to join the London Tweed Run—a ride that's all about style!

Riders wear tweed suits, vintage hats, and bow ties as they pedal through the city. The ride is about 13.5 miles (21.7 km) long. But the cyclists are in no rush. They even stop for tea and lunch partway through the ride! It's not a race but a parade that celebrates bygone times and retro charm. But for those who like to win, there are prizes for best vintage bicycle and best mustache!

Soaked Sahara

In September 2024, parts of the Sahara—one of the driest places on Earth—flooded! In southeast Morocco, heavy storms brought up to 8 inches (20.3 cm) of rain in just two days. Some of the flooding created new lakes and even submerged palm trees! The rare rain made for interesting landscapes, but it also led to dangerous flooding in some towns. Scientists believe climate change could mean more heavy rain in the Sahara in the future.

SUNKEN Supper

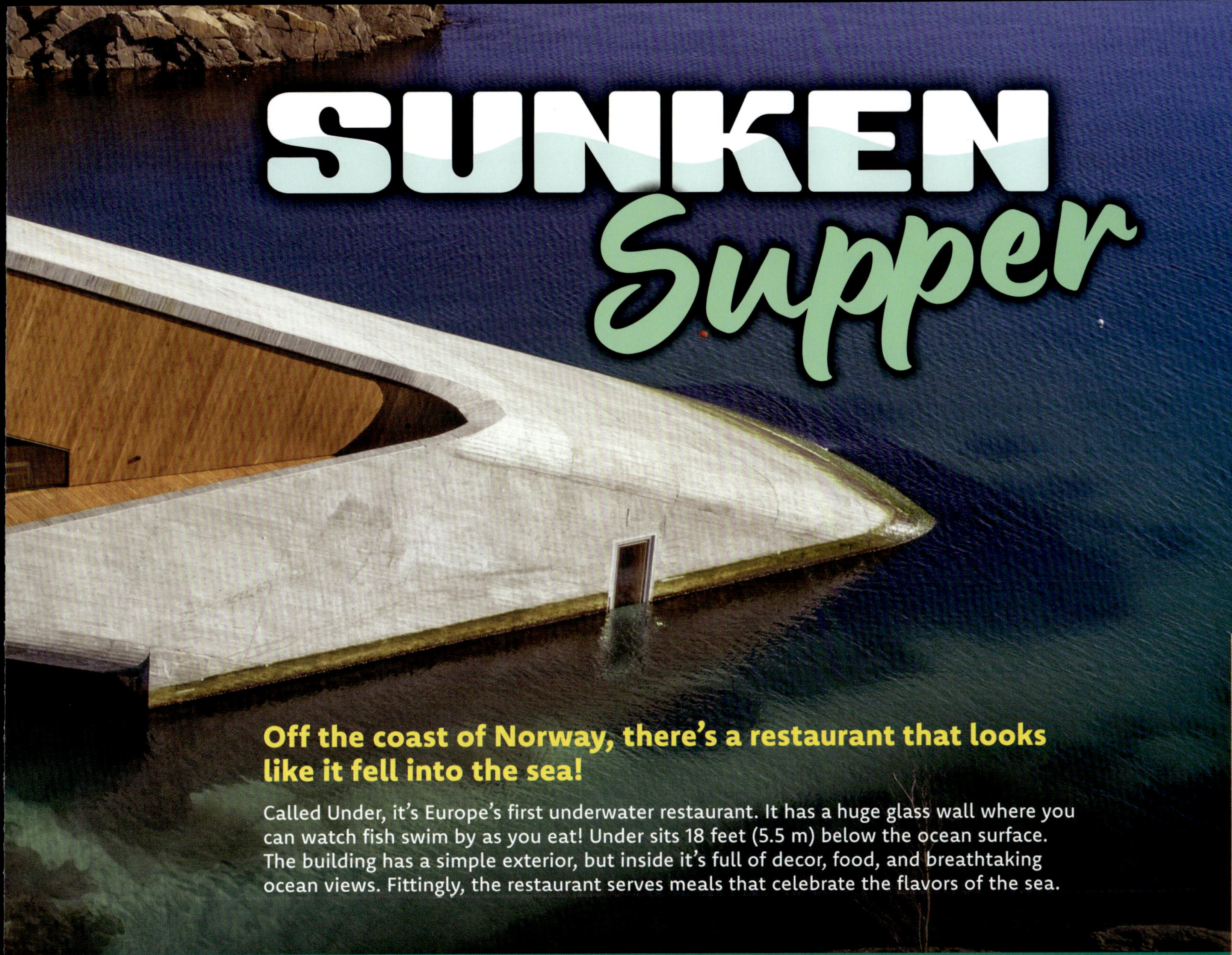

Off the coast of Norway, there's a restaurant that looks like it fell into the sea!

Called Under, it's Europe's first underwater restaurant. It has a huge glass wall where you can watch fish swim by as you eat! Under sits 18 feet (5.5 m) below the ocean surface. The building has a simple exterior, but inside it's full of decor, food, and breathtaking ocean views. Fittingly, the restaurant serves meals that celebrate the flavors of the sea.

Pretty Fly

Nevada's Fly Geyser is a colorful natural-ish wonder—made by accident! Back in 1964, a company drilled a well for hot water. The problem? They didn't close it properly and hot water started shooting out. Over time, minerals from the water built up and formed colorful mounds that are nearly 6 feet (1.8 m) tall! Covered in algae, they still shoot water into the air today. What's even more amazing is that quartz crystals are growing inside the mounds. Quartz usually takes thousands of years to form in a geyser!

HOOKED UP

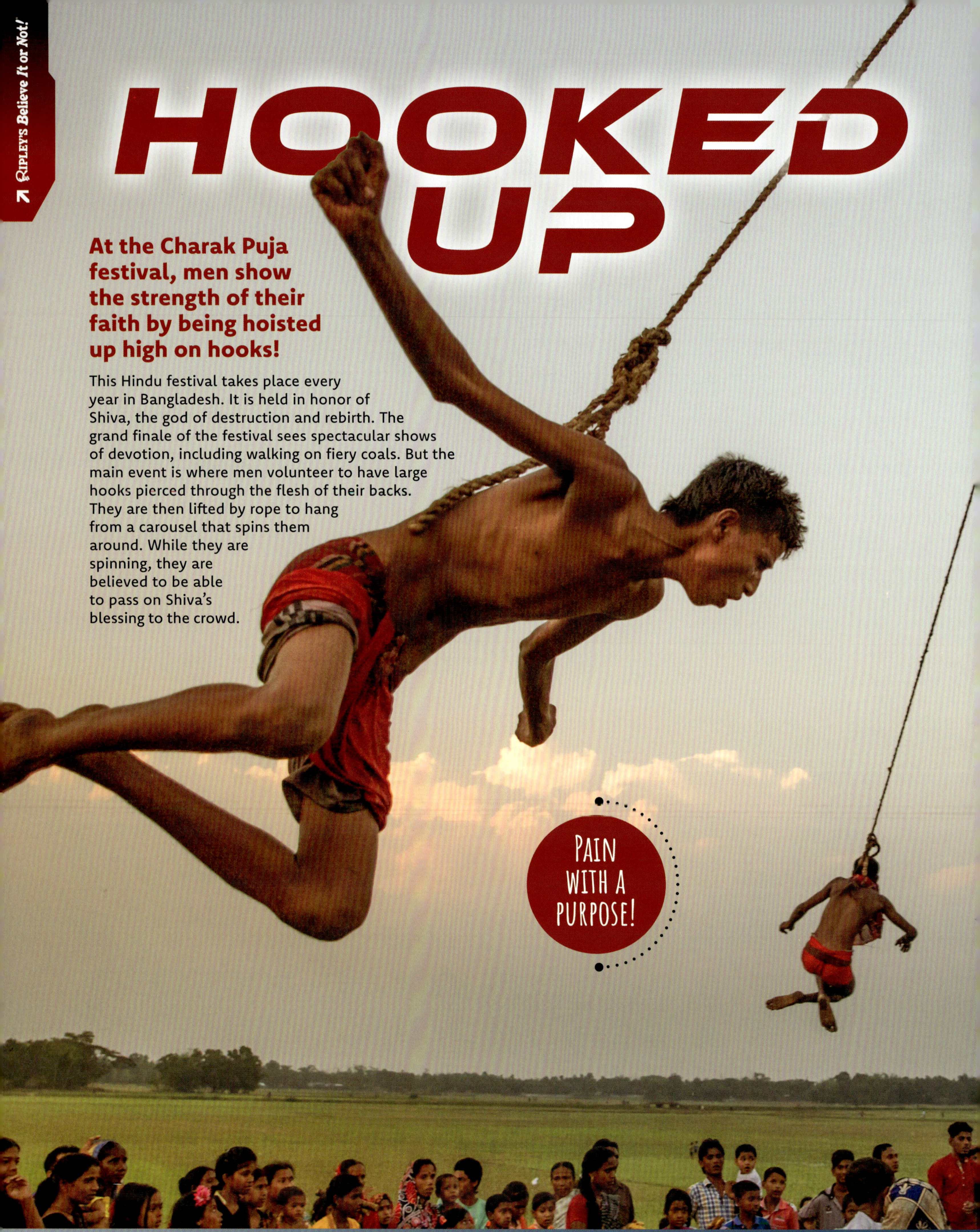

At the Charak Puja festival, men show the strength of their faith by being hoisted up high on hooks!

This Hindu festival takes place every year in Bangladesh. It is held in honor of Shiva, the god of destruction and rebirth. The grand finale of the festival sees spectacular shows of devotion, including walking on fiery coals. But the main event is where men volunteer to have large hooks pierced through the flesh of their backs. They are then lifted by rope to hang from a carousel that spins them around. While they are spinning, they are believed to be able to pass on Shiva's blessing to the crowd.

PAIN WITH A PURPOSE!

FAMILY BUSINESS ↗ The Raeapteek pharmacy in Tallinn, Estonia, has been in the same building for more than 600 years. It was founded in the early fifteenth century. It was later owned by the Burchart family for more than 325 years. During that time, it was run by 10 generations of Burchart sons named Johann. The family sold the pharmacy in 1911 following the death of Johann X Burchart.

BIRD CALLS ↗ An old pay phone in Takoma Park, Maryland, only makes bird calls. It was created by artist David Schulman. Callers can press any button on the keypad to hear the different sounds of local birds, from a kingfisher to a crow.

DEEP TRAP

A sand trap at the Royal St. George's Golf Club in Sandwich, England, is 40 feet (12.2 m) deep. That makes it more than six times the height of the average player. The Himalaya trap on the fourth hole was created by a bomb during World War II.

HUGE VESSEL ↗ The *Höegh Aurora*, a Chinese-built container vessel operating in Norway, can hold 9,100 cars. Measuring 655.8 feet (199.9 m) long and 123 feet (37.5 m) wide, it has 14 decks. It also uses renewable energy, with 16,145.9 square feet (1,500 sq m) of solar panels on the top deck. They reduce electricity production from the ship's generators.

HAIR FESTIVAL ↗ The Australian town of Kurri Kurri holds an annual contest to find the best mullet haircut. A mullet hairstyle is one where the hair is cut shorter on the front and sides and longer in the back. The Mulletfest attracts entrants from all over the world, including the United States, the UK, and Canada. It is watched by more than 8,000 people.

TRUCKER Paradise

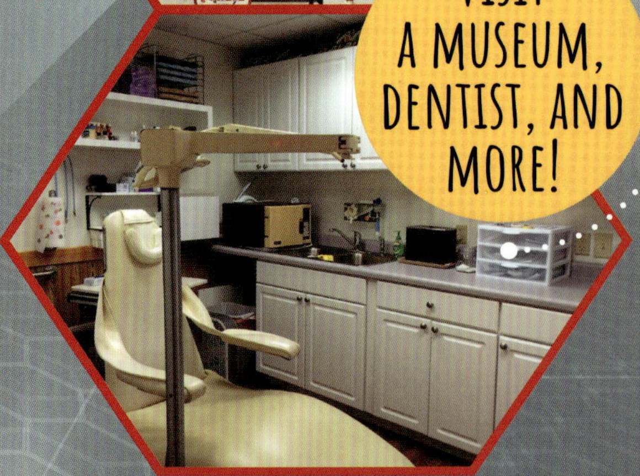

VISIT A MUSEUM, DENTIST, AND MORE!

With more than 1,000 parking spots, Iowa 80 claims to be the world's largest truck stop!

Located in Walcott, Iowa, this interstate stop is like a small city for travelers. Open since 1964, it's packed with all kinds of shops. It even has a dentist, chiropractor, and hair salon. For history fans, the Iowa 80 Trucking Museum is a must-see. Drivers can eat in one of nine restaurants, take a shower, or stop by the movie theater—and then simply carry on with their journey. It's the ultimate pit stop for truckers and makes for a memorable day out!

TRUCK STOP TIDBITS

About **6,000 customers** visit Iowa 80 each day.

Iowa 80 has served over **36 million cups of coffee** since it opened.

Iowa 80 hosts the Walcott Truckers Jamboree—more than **45,000 people** attended in 2025!

Each year, Iowa 80 cooks roughly **50 tons of potatoes** for hungry visitors.

Iowa 80 has **900 parking spots** for trucks.

Over **23 million eggs** have been fried, poached, or scrambled at Iowa 80.

Viking Crossing

Aarhus in Denmark doesn't have normal green and red crosswalk lights—they're pictures of Vikings! To celebrate the city's Viking heritage, 17 sets of special lights have been installed. Some of the green lights for "go" show a Viking running, wielding their ax. Some of the red lights for "stop" show a Viking holding up a shield and their hand.

Head Home

Every November, people in Bolivia join the Día de las Ñatitas festival to honor the human skulls they keep in their homes!

The skulls—called ñatitas—are like extra family members. They even have names! It is believed that the skull spirits bring good luck and health. Sometimes the skulls come from family members. But many come from complete strangers! On the day of the festival, the ñatitas are decorated and carried to La Paz Cemetery in a parade of singing and dancing. After, they are placed back in their special spot in the home!

CHEESY PREDICTIONS ↗ Tyromancy is the practice of telling people's fortunes through cheese. It began in the second century. It is done by studying the smell, patterns, and texture of cheese, especially veined blue cheese.

HOFF MUSEUM ↗ There is a museum in Berlin, Germany, dedicated to U.S. actor and *Baywatch* star David Hasselhoff. Its mural of "The Hoff" originally featured a patch of fake chest hair. But the museum removed it as visitors kept on touching it.

COLOSSAL CORAL ↗ A single piece of undersea coral located off the Solomon Islands in the South Pacific is so big it can be seen from space. It measures 111.5 feet (34 m) wide and 105 feet (32 m) long. That makes it the size of two basketball courts placed side by side.

HAIR TREE

A family tree made of human hair is on display at the Old State Capitol in Frankfort, Kentucky. It was created by Mary Stout in the mid-nineteenth century using brown hair from the Cardwell family of Shelby County.

BONE CHINA ↗ Customers at a New York farm restaurant eat from dishware made from the leftover bones of the farm's own cows. The restaurant is called Blue Hill at Stone Barns and is located in Pocantico Hills. The plates and bowls are handcrafted by Pennsylvania artist Gregg Moore.

FOOT BEATING ↗ At Korean weddings, the groom's friends and family remove his shoes and beat the soles of his feet with a cane or dried fish. This ritual is known as *falaka*. It is seen as a final trial of strength and character for the groom before he takes his new bride home.

WATER SLIDE ↗ A water slide spirals down the side of Puhuasi Mountain in Lishui, China. The slide is 8,934 feet (2,723.1 m) long—that's nearly 2 miles (3.2 km)!

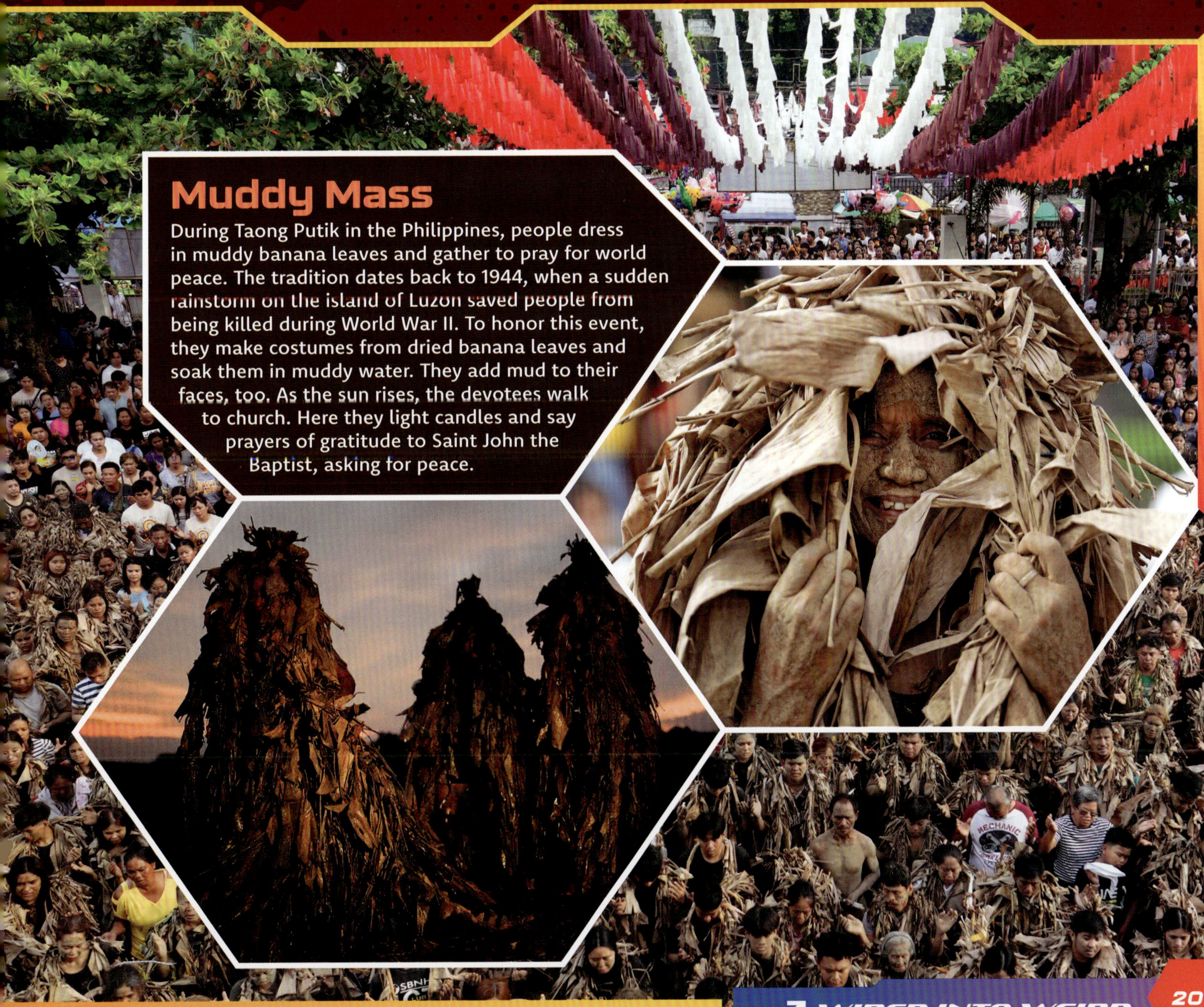

Muddy Mass

During Taong Putik in the Philippines, people dress in muddy banana leaves and gather to pray for world peace. The tradition dates back to 1944, when a sudden rainstorm on the island of Luzon saved people from being killed during World War II. To honor this event, they make costumes from dried banana leaves and soak them in muddy water. They add mud to their faces, too. As the sun rises, the devotees walk to church. Here they light candles and say prayers of gratitude to Saint John the Baptist, asking for peace.

Village Dummies

Tired of living in a ghost town, the residents of Ichinono, Japan, filled their village with life-size puppets!

Dozens of the dummies can be found across the town doing everyday things. There's a family gathering wood, kids playing on swings, and even farmers looking at the fields. The puppets are made from fabric and mannequins. Each one is dressed in old clothes, including shirts, dresses, and sweaters. It's thought there might be more puppets than people in the small village. As of 2024, there were less than 60 humans living there!

NOT THE MOST TALKATIVE NEIGHBORS

Step Up

In a traditional dance known as Magunatip, people dance while bamboo poles are moved around their feet! The bamboo dance is a tradition of the Murut people from Malaysia. Performers jump in and out of clapping bamboo poles—without getting trapped. The dancers and pole movers must be in perfect sync with each other. Music and the sound of gongs help them keep pace. The dance was once used in rituals to scare evil spirits away or to welcome warriors home. Now it's a treasured part of the culture.

ROUND EGG ↗ Ali Greene, a farmworker in England, was left feeling shell-shocked after discovering a one-in-a-billion egg. Instead of being oval-shaped, it was perfectly round. She has processed more than 30,000 eggs, but this one was *egg*-straordinary. It attracted her attention because its unusual shape stopped it from falling through the hole from the conveyor belt to the trays.

ANCIENT GAME ↗ The game of Rock Paper Scissors originated in China around 2,000 years ago. Its previous names include "frog, slug, snake" and "fox, village head, hunter."

SNAIL MAIL ↗ In 2024, a postcard was finally delivered to a bank in Swansea, Wales, 121 years after it was mailed. The card had been mailed on August 3, 1903, and bore a King Edward VII stamp.

NEW ACCENT ↗ A week after undergoing jaw surgery in 2021, Kim Hall suddenly started speaking in a strange accent. She comes from Australia but found herself speaking in a northern English accent. And she has kept it ever since—even though she has never been to the UK. It is a case of foreign accent syndrome, a rare medical condition. It has even left her struggling to pronounce some Australian words.

Speedy Shovels

At the yearly Shovel Races hosted by Angel Fire Ski Resort in New Mexico, people speed down a mountain at around 60 mph (96.6 kmph) while riding on a grain shovel! They simply sit on the shovel head, hold on to the handle, and let gravity pull them down the slope. It only takes about 15 seconds to reach the finish line! Shovel racing began in the 1970s. At the end of a tiring shift, lift operators wanted to get down the mountain fast—so they jumped on their shovels!

Floating Fancy

On Dal Lake in Srinagar, India, there are more than 900 houseboats! They were first built in the nineteenth century by British lords. At the time, foreigners were not allowed to own homes on land. Houseboats were a clever loophole. Today, many of the floating homes are used as luxury hotels. While the houseboats are a big draw for tourists, their popularity has also caused a lot of pollution in Dal Lake.

STRAW BUNDLE Bundles of straw can sometimes be seen hanging under bridges crossing the River Thames in London, England. They are put there to warn ships of any reduction in headroom beneath the bridge during maintenance work. The bylaw dates back centuries but is still used today.

PINEAPPLE CHARGE Do you think pineapple belongs on a pizza? Well, the owners of Lupa Pizza in Norwich, England, clearly don't think so. To discourage customers from ordering a Hawaiian, they charged an extra $155 for anyone wanting to add pineapple to their regular $20 pizzas.

COLD SURFING Surfing takes place all year round at Lofoten, Norway, even though it is located 99.4 miles (160 km) above the Arctic Circle. There is often snow on the beach in winter—and the water temperature can be as low as 39°F (3.9°C).

Seaweed Struggle

Picture-perfect vacations on beautiful Caribbean beaches are being ruined by smelly seaweed! Brown algae called sargassum has piled up along the shores. There's about 38 million tons of it. Scientists aren't sure why there has been so much in recent years. Some think it could be caused by changes in climate and currents. Sargassum doesn't just reek; it also smothers sea creatures and blocks sunlight from coral reefs. There's so much of the stuff that sometimes heavy machinery is needed to move it out of the way!

DARING DIVE

Every year, brave divers leap from cliffs as tall as buildings for the International Waterfall Jumping Competition!

The competition is hosted by the country of Bosnia and Herzegovina. In 2025, it was held in the town of Jajce at the Pliva Waterfall, which is 65.6 feet (20 m) high! Daring to take the plunge were 16 divers from around the world. They performed a traditional kind of jump called a Lasta, or "swallow." They leap with their arms extended to the side, rather than out front, bringing them together right before they enter the water. The judges held up signs with their score out of 10 after each jump.

JUST PASSING THROUGH

There's a train track in Chongqing, China, that runs straight through a 19-story building!

The monorail at Liziba Station goes through the sixth to eighth floors. The floors above the station are apartments. The building is designed to reduce noise, so the trains don't disturb people who live there. Also in the building is a museum which includes the city's rail history. The setup has turned Liziba into a local hot spot. Tourists visit just to see the train pass through the building!

ALL ABOARD!

Dead Center

When Nancy Kerlin Barnett died in 1831, she was buried on a small hill with a view of a creek. Fast forward 70 years and her grave turned out to be the perfect spot for a road! At first the grave was going to be moved, but Nancy's grandson put up a fight. Instead, the road was built around her grave! The grave site has since been rebuilt to make it safer, and the workers found the bones of six other people. A plaque and road sign now mark where Nancy rests peacefully with her family.

Camo Calls

When is a tree not a tree? When it's a cell tower! Billions of people use cell phones every day, connecting to a wireless network created by cell towers. Unfortunately, cell towers are really tall and not exactly pretty. To help hide these eyesores, many towers are camouflaged to blend in with their surroundings. They are often made to look like trees, but some have been disguised as cacti, water towers, and even church steeples! Have you ever spotted one of these hidden cell towers?

WIDE LOAD

PERFECT TIME ↗ The Aether Clock OC 020 is so precise it would take about 10 billion years for it to be wrong by even a single second. The Japanese-made clock costs over $3 million.

SQUARE COFFIN ↗ When she died in 1714, the body of Queen Anne of England and Scotland became very swollen. In fact, she was so bloated that she had to be buried in a square coffin.

MILKY FROG ↗ Before fridges were invented, some farmers in Finland and Russia would drop live frogs into their milk buckets to keep the milk from spoiling!

Split Sea

A few times a year in South Korea, the Jindo Sea parts and reveals a path across the ocean floor! The path is about 2 miles (3.2 km) long. The phenomenon lasts for around an hour. During this time, thousands of tourists get to walk between the waves to the island of Modo. The event is actually a super low tide. It happens here because of the land's shape and how the tides work—just for that hour!

ANCIENT CHEESE ↗ A 3,600-year-old cheese was discovered on the neck of a Chinese mummy. The mummy's coffin was opened during excavations in 2003. More than 20 years later, the substance that had been laid across the mummified young woman was identified by scientists as kefir cheese.

STILL KICKING ↗ In March 2025, Bulgarian soccer club Arda Kardzhali held a minute of silence to mourn the death of their former player Petko Ganchev. Before a game with rival club Levski Sofia, players from both teams stood in the center circle and bowed their heads. The crowd was hushed. It was all very respectful. The only problem? Ganchev was very much alive! When they realized they had made a mistake, Arda apologized.

FISHY PROTEST ↗ There are many reasons why soccer games are paused. It is usually for a bad injury or an emergency among the spectators. But a league game in Norway was suspended after angry fans threw fish cakes onto the field! They were protesting about the use of a video assistant referee.

When Kiruna Church in Sweden was at risk of sinking, the whole building was rolled to a new home 3.1 miles (5 km) away!

A trolley with more than 220 wheels was built to handle the 672-ton church. On moving day, the building was blessed by the vicar before starting its journey. Traveling at just 0.3 mph (0.5 kmph), it took two days to reach its new location, still in Kiruna. The 113-year-old church was wider than the roads, so lampposts and signs also had to be moved to allow the church to pass!

Air Archive

Scientists in Tasmania have been collecting air samples for nearly 50 years! But not just any old air. The samples are collected at a special station located in Cape Grim. The air there is as clean as can be because it travels thousands of miles across the ocean before it arrives. New samples are taken up to six times a year. An "air archive" of the samples contains 170 cylinders. Each one is like a moment frozen in time. This important scientific collection can be used to compare air quality across decades.

EXHIBIT NO. 174067

Spikey Shoes

These metal shoes are anything but ordinary. They are a medieval torture device that has tiny holes where spikes were placed. A person would have to stand on their tiptoes to avoid the spikes! If they put weight on their heel, the spikes would puncture their foot. These shoes were often worn while someone was on a pillory, which is a device that has holes to lock someone's head and hands into place.

SEE MORE!

STAY ON YOUR TOES, OR ELSE YOU GET SPIKED IN THE HEELS!

EXHIBIT NO. 7592

One Tough Nut

This neat little tool is used to cut betel nuts! The nut, which just so happens to be a berry, is popular throughout Asia. It has a tough outer shell that makes it hard to crack. Therefore, a special type of scissors was created to help break the nut down into small, chewable pieces.

FACT FILES

The cassowary is a giant, flightless bird. It's one of the most dangerous birds in the world, due to its sharp claws!

EXHIBIT NO. 8563

Bird Blade

People native to New Guinea would create weapons from the bones of the cassowary bird! Sharp and decorated with intricate carvings, the daggers could be used in close combat.

AROUND THE WORLD

UP NEXT...

BEYOND BELIEF

MODEL STUDENT The bronze sculpture in Cambridge, Massachusetts, of John Harvard, founder of Harvard University, is not of Harvard himself because nobody knew what he looked like. So in 1883—245 years after Harvard's death—sculptor Daniel Chester French asked a Harvard student named Sherman Hoar to sit as a model for the head.

OLD AIRPORT The town of Bar Nunn, Wyoming, was an airport until 1952. Its extra-wide streets are the former runways and taxiways of the old Wardwell Field Airport.

PEANUTS APLENTY It takes about 540 peanuts to make a 12-ounce (340.2-g) jar of peanut butter.

BOX BUILDING In New York City, there is a 550-foot-tall (167.6-m) skyscraper that has no windows.

POOP PACKAGE

Customs agents at Minneapolis-Saint Paul International Airport in Minnesota seized a box of giraffe poop from a passenger from Iowa. She had collected it on a trip to Kenya and wanted to make a necklace from it.

COMPLAINER CAFÉ Mori Ouchi, a café in Tokyo, Japan, caters only to pessimists. It was opened in 2020 during the COVID-19 pandemic, when people were feeling particularly negative about life.

TWIN TOWNS The town of Ulverston, England, where comedian Stan Laurel was born, is officially twinned with Harlem, Georgia, the birthplace of his screen partner, Oliver Hardy.

NAPKIN DESIGN Seattle's Space Needle was first designed on a napkin in a café by hotel executive Edward E. Carlson. He was inspired by a similar structure he had seen on a 1959 trip to Stuttgart, Germany.

LONG HAIR Macie Davis-Southerland from California has a single arm hair that measures 7.2 inches (18.3 cm) long.

READY FOR Takeoff

Inventor Jean-Pierre David longed to fly like a bird—so he made it happen with the Aéroplume!

And now anyone can try it! One of the places people can fly Aéroplume is Salamander Cave in France. First, an instructor helps you into a harness underneath the helium-filled balloon. This leaves you lying face down, ready to take off. You grasp the wing handles and flap, flap, flap like a bird; then up you go! The balloon can go forward, backward, left, and right. After soaring around the cave for 20 minutes, you simply glide down to land!

Dark Hedges

In Northern Ireland there's a road lined with beech trees that looks like it leads to another world! Known as the Dark Hedges, this twisted tree tunnel was planted almost 250 years ago to impress visitors. Now it's one of the most photographed places in the country—and it was even featured in *Game of Thrones!* The trees bend and stretch like they're alive. Walk through at sunrise, and the glowing trees make you feel like you're in a dream! But as the sun sets, the atmosphere turns moody and eerie.

Trotting TRAVELERS

In the Great Northern Gallop in New Zealand, people race alongside miniature horses!

The race takes place once a year. Participants can be assigned a miniature pony or bring their own. The four-day event covers roughly 62 miles (99.8 km). The course is as unique as its runners! It has both a sandy beach as well as a charming forest. Born to Run Adventure Racing puts on the event. Their goal is to have a fun race and support the welfare of the adorable ponies.

RACING WITH A MINIATURE PONY THROUGH ALL TERRAIN!

Precious Cargo

Some donkeys wear special coats with lamb-sized pockets to help carry baby sheep down mountains! Every year, shepherds in Italy move sheep from the mountains down to the plains to graze. The journey can take as many as 20 days! But what about the newborn lambs? They can't walk that far. That's where the donkeys step in! Shepherds have been using donkeys or mules this way for many years. They make good "nannies" because they're patient and protective of their cargo.

LOCKED IN ↗ In 2023, three men broke into a decommissioned jail in St. Louis, Missouri, but accidentally locked themselves inside a cell. They had to call 911, and after being freed, they were promptly arrested.

DIAMOND DISCOVERY ↗ A diamond ring worth more than $800,000 that went missing from a Malaysian businesswoman's hotel room at the Ritz in Paris, France, was later discovered in the bag of a vacuum cleaner.

MESSI NAPKIN ↗ In 2000, Spanish soccer club Barcelona agreed to sign then 13-year-old Lionel Messi in a meeting using a plain white paper napkin. The napkin sold at auction in 2024 for around $965,540.

TRAGIC COINCIDENCE ↗ There have only been three Major League Baseball players in history named Aurelio: Aurelio Monteagudo, Aurelio López, and Aurelio Rodriguez. All three died in car accidents between the ages of 44 and 52.

GIFT WRAP ↗ Each holiday season, people in the UK use 227,000 miles (365,321.1 km) of wrapping paper—almost the distance from Earth to the Moon.

FLAG CHANGES ↗ The design of the U.S. flag has been amended 26 times since 1777.

STOMACH SOUNDS ↗ The scientific name for the sound of a rumbling stomach is "borborygmus." It is the sound made by the movement of food, fluid, and gas in the intestines.

NEO TO THE RESCUE!

Poodle Patrol

Neo uses his best doggy paddle to rescue swimmers on a beach near Malaga, Spain! The snowy white poodle helps lifeguards bring struggling swimmers back to shore. Neo wears a colorful life vest when reporting for duty. He gets sunscreen added to his nose to protect him from the sun, and then he is ready for some saving! The fluffy poodle is not alone when on the job. He's on a team with four Labradors!

APPRECIATION DAY **NOVEMBER 17** ↗ NATIONAL

ICY Stay

In the Alps, you can stay in a hotel made out of snow and ice!

The Iglu-Dorf hotel chain creates igloo ice villages that melt away every year. They are built in Switzerland, Austria, and Germany. Artists come from all over the world to decorate the walls inside. You might find a playful monster around the corner or an owl with its wings spread wide, welcoming you to the icy room. Some igloos have a hot tub to warm up in if you are feeling a little frozen. And even the beds are made of ice! Each guest gets a sleeping bag for the night and is welcomed with a warm tea in the morning.

Fur Real?

In December 1960, famous explorer Sir Edmund Hillary met some monks in Nepal who believed they had part of a 300-year-old yeti scalp! They kept it in a small glass box inside their temple and believed it gave the village good luck. Curious, Sir Edmund asked to take the scalp to London so it could be studied. The village offered him a deal: Sir Edmund could take the scalp if he donated to their school and let someone from the village go with him to watch over the scalp. Sir Edmund agreed. Sadly, scientists concluded the scalp was really from a goat-like animal called a serow. The scalp was then returned to the temple, where it remains to this day.

PROOF THAT YETI EXIST?

A COOL PLACE TO CHILL OUT!

STONEHENGE SNUB ↗ In 1915, Cecil Chubb purchased ancient English monument Stonehenge as a surprise gift for his wife. He paid about $8,000, but she didn't like it very much, so three years later he gave it to the nation.

HISTORIC RESTAURANT ↗ Cole's Hearth Room, a restaurant in Palmyra, Missouri, is a former farmhouse that served as a hospital during the U.S. Civil War and later as a cemetery caretaker's residence.

COFFEE CLEANER ↗ In the tenth century, 500 years before it first became popular as a drink, coffee was used for cleaning and freshening hands.

ISLAND HOP ↗ Over a period of four years, Ken Fowler sailed solo around all 262 islands off the English and Welsh coasts in a boat just 13 feet (4 m) long.

WORLD'S WORST ↗ For more than 40 years, Blythefield Country Club in Grand Rapids, Michigan, has held an annual golf tournament that awards special prizes to players with the *highest* score. It is named after Maurice Flitcroft, an English crane operator who had never played a round of golf before scoring a 49 over par (or 121) while failing to qualify for the 1976 British Open. He became known as the world's worst golfer.

JENGA GENIUS ↗ Auldin Maxwell, a 15-year-old from British Columbia, Canada, stacked 1,840 Jenga blocks on a single vertical block.

VINTAGE BEER ↗ Dylan McDonnell from Utah used an ancient papyrus document recipe to recreate a beer that was brewed 3,500 years ago in Egypt. The ingredients for his Sinai Sour beer included sycamore figs, golden raisins, frankincense, and 3,000-year-old yeast.

Going Bear-Foot

Fashion brand H&M released a pair of heels covered in long faux fur! Put them on and voilà—you have high-heeled "bear" feet! Some people love the cozy, quirky look, while others think they are a bit strange. These shoes are not recommended for a rainy day, though, as wet fur is never in fashion! Whether you think they're cool or un-*bear*-able, these furry shoes have everyone talking.

RIPLEY'S COLLECTION

EXHIBIT NO. 21412

Perfect Fit

This strange-looking gadget helps hatmakers measure their customers' noggins! Known as a conformateur or conformer, it was invented in France in the 1800s. It is made up of dozens of spring-loaded bars that move when placed on someone's head. At the top of each bar is a small point. The hatmaker stamps a piece of paper through the points, creating a perfect template of that person's head size!

SEE MORE!

STANDING STILL

Over 1,000 eerie figures stand in a Finnish field—silent, still, and strange!

Known as the *Silent People*, they're each made from two pieces of wood and have peat heads covered in straw. The heads don't have faces but seem to be staring in the same direction. Each figure wears donated clothing that is changed twice a year. In the wintertime, the figures are even dressed in coats. Finnish artist Reijo Kela created the art piece in the 1980s, but he never revealed the meaning behind it.

NOT GOING THERE AT NIGHT!

CAR FUNERAL ↗ The Polara family of Gujarat, India, spent more than $4,500 on a funeral for their 18-year-old car. They didn't want to send their faithful old Suzuki Wagon to a scrapyard. Instead, they arranged a lavish burial ceremony, attended by 1,500 people. The SUV was decorated with flower petals and colorful garlands. Then it was covered with green cloth and lowered into a 15-foot-deep (4.6-m) grave. The family even built a shrine for the vehicle.

DEVIL'S MONUMENT ↗ 666 is often called the devil's number. So perhaps it's no surprise that the Fountain of the Fallen Angel in Madrid, Spain, stands exactly 666 meters—or 2,185 feet—above sea level. It is reputed to be the only prominent sculpture in the world dedicated to the devil.

SAD SUMMIT ↗ Mount Disappointment in Victoria, Australia, was named in 1824 by British explorers Hamilton Hume and William Hovell. They came up with the name because they were disappointed that they were unable to see Port Phillip Bay from the mountain's 2,608.3-foot-high (795-m) summit.

TOP SECRET ↗ There is something unique about the Starbucks inside the CIA headquarters in Langley, Virginia. It is the only Starbucks in the world that won't ask for your name with your order. That's because the people working at the heart of U.S. intelligence need to remain anonymous.

GHOST MARRIAGE ↗ Among the Nuer people of South Sudan, if a groom dies before his wedding he can be replaced by another man. This custom is known as a ghost marriage. Any resulting children are considered to belong to the dead man.

SANDWICH LOVERS ↗ The average person in Britain eats 18,304 sandwiches in their lifetime.

CHRISTIAN & SCOOBY

Christian Stoinev and his dogs wow crowds with their amazing act that combines circus stunts and cute tricks!

The dogs, called Percy and Milo, can do things like balance on basketballs, jump through hoops, and stand on Christian's feet as he performs a handstand! But how did this act even start? As a teen growing up in the circus, Christian got a pet dog named Scooby. It turned out the pup had a talent for balancing! They trained and were soon performing together. That was more than 12 years ago. Christian has since added more dogs to his family. Today the group does about 50 acts a year, often at basketball halftime shows. Percy and Milo perform under the stage name "Scooby" to carry on his legacy.

BALANCED ON ONE ARM!

CHIHUA-WOW!

PANORAMIC SKY-HIGH VIEWS!

High Home

Off the coast of Cornwall, England, there sits a house on top of a 70-foot-tall (21.3-m) rock! During high tide, it's surrounded by water. The house can only be reached by crossing a tiny suspension bridge. The spot is rented out to guests who can brave the walkway. Once you cross, it's like staying on your own private island. The sight is breathtaking, with a 360-degree panoramic view of the ocean at high tide.

UNCRACKABLE CODE ↗ Two coded handwritten notes hidden in a nineteenth-century silk bustle dress took 10 years and 170 codebooks to crack. The secret notes were discovered in 2013 but weren't deciphered until 2023. Wayne Chan, a research computer analyst at the University of Manitoba, figured out that the code represented weather observations for the United States and Canada from 1888.

RICH RIVER ↗ A fire at Rockwood & Company's chocolate factory in Brooklyn on May 12, 1919, caused a river of chocolate to flow down nearby streets. It collected in storm drains, prompting crowds of children to rush from miles around to scoop it up with their fingers.

WRONG NUMBER ↗ Nicole Paulino of Gaithersburg, Maryland, was shocked when she applied to renew her driver's license. According to official records, she was dead! The mistake occurred because a funeral home had incorrectly recorded a deceased person's Social Security number. They had accidentally typed in Paulino's number instead.

Dolls for Days

Milena Przybylski from Germany owns around 900 Monster High dolls! She started collecting them in 2010. She has every doll ever released, plus a few special ones. Milena likes that the dolls are all about being unique and accepting others. She loves to share her dolls with the world and would like to open a museum one day. But Milena's greatest wish? To have a Monster High doll that looks just like her!

GARDEN GROTTO

Francis Proctor from Southport, England, spent almost 30 years digging a cave in his backyard!

The tunnels and cave go about 20 feet (6.1 m) underground. Francis did the work himself using simple tools. It started as a hobby and grew into an entire hidden world. His late wife Barbara helped him along the way. She used her knowledge as a mathematician to help bring Francis's vision to life. His garden above ground is also impressive. It has a waterfall, a bridge, and even an Easter Island head. Want to see for yourself? Francis often opens his garden grotto to the public!

CAVE UNDERGROUND TO GARDEN ABOVE!

MOSAIC MAKEOVER

Just outside of Havana, Cuba, a village has been turned into art!

Artist José Rodríguez Fuster transformed the seaside village of Jaimanitas. He started work in the 1970s on his own house. He added tiles to the outer walls to make a mosaic. The neighborhood loved his work, so he kept going! There are now more than 80 buildings covered in art. Each building has its own unique style. It's a real-life rainbow village, and it's been nicknamed "Fusterlandia!" Visitors come from all over the world to see it.

José Rodríguez Fuster

A COLORFUL PLACE TO LIVE!

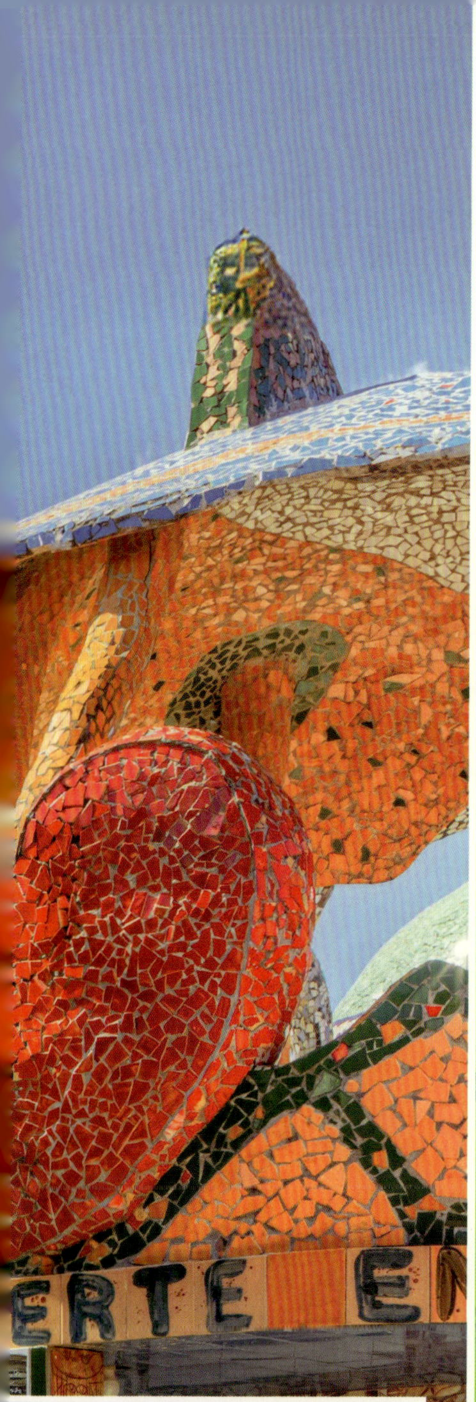

YOU GOTTA CHECK THESE BOOKS OUT!

BEYOND BELIEF

Leafing Through

At a xylotheque, you can explore a forest without leaving the room! A xylotheque is like a library, but instead of books with pages, it's filled with "books" made from wood. These wooden books come from different kinds of trees. Some of the tree books can be opened. Inside, you might find samples of bark, leaves, seeds, or tiny branches. Some even have wax versions of the tree's fruit! Scientists and nature lovers use these special libraries to learn about trees from all over the world.

Lickety SPLIT

At the Ekamai Mall in Bangkok, Thailand, dozens of feisty felines went paw to paw in the Cat Lick Championship!

Each cat went as fast as they could to slurp up a tasty treat. The fastest cat finished in an impressive 20 seconds! Some of the felines were even dressed up while competing. The competition was part of the Pet Fun Fest, a weekend packed with pet-themed activities. There was a pet fashion show, a dog marathon, and even the Cat Olympics.

KIMMON, THE CAT LICK CHAMP!

Pet Passport

JJ Yosh, from Colorado, travels the world with the *purr*-fect companion—his cat Simon! The two have covered over 300,000 miles (482,803.2 km) since starting their adventure. They have already been to multiple countries. Everywhere they go, the pair is always doing thrilling activities! From white water rafting to rock climbing, Simon takes part. If Simon gets tired or needs to be safer, JJ carries him on his shoulders. This is why the black cat quickly earned the nickname "Backpacking Kitty."

Tabby Tour

Every year, hundreds of people gather in a Minneapolis, Minnesota, neighborhood for the Wedge Live! Cat Tour. They wander for several miles just to take a look at the local cats! The crowds can't get enough of the whiskered royalty that lounges behind the windows. Some owners put up posters outside their homes describing their cats. Some even bring the furry stars outside to meet their fans! The event started in 2017 when a resident who took snaps of neighborhood cats while on walks realized others might enjoy it, too!

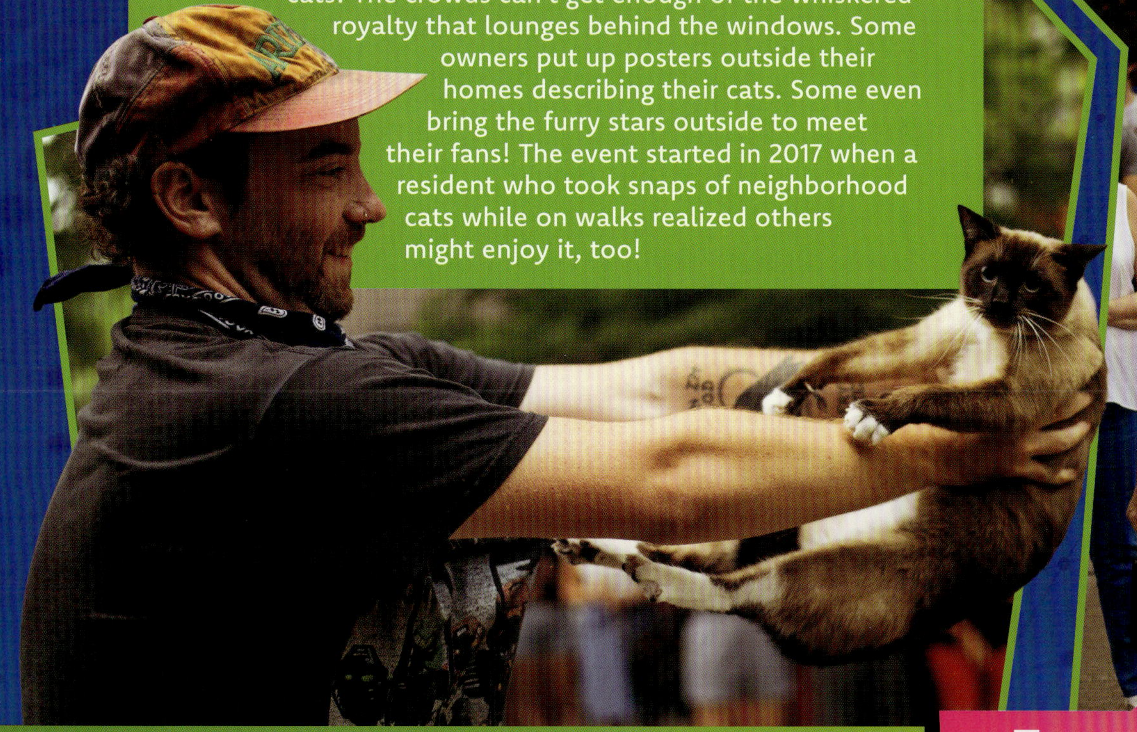

I Dough

For their wedding, Texas couple Beth and Brandon Duhon ordered a giant 8-foot (2.4-m) pizza! The pie was prepped by local company Dirt Road Cookers. The wedding party added toppings like pepperoni and peppers. Six people were needed to lift the hefty order into the oven! Soon the dough began to rise and a perfect pizza took shape. A giant pizza cutter was used to slice up the pie. What an unforgettable feast for a special day!

GOLF TEST ↗ A golf store in London, England, wanted to make sure that a new line of designer shoes was only bought by genuine golfers. So they only sold the Air Jordan 1 Low Golf x Travis Scott shoes to customers who proved they could hit a ball at least 200 yards (150 yards for women). Every prospective buyer was given two attempts to hit a ball that distance.

WHEELBARROW RACER ↗ Dylan Phillips, a mechanic from Wales, built a motorized garden wheelbarrow that can reach speeds of 52 mph (83.7 kmph).

LONG RALLY ↗ Swedes Emil Ohlsson and Fredrik Nilsson played a nonstop table tennis rally that lasted for 13 hours, 37 minutes, and 6 seconds.

SHELTERED LIFE ↗ Mihailo Tolotos, a Greek Orthodox monk, died at age 82 without ever seeing a woman. He lived his entire life (c. 1855–1938) in the monastery on Mount Athos. Women are forbidden from setting foot on Mount Athos.

WINNER OF THE FIRST WIENIE 500 RACE!

Frank and Furious

In May 2025, six 27-foot-long (8.2-m) hot-dog buses took to the Indianapolis Motor Speedway to race against each other! Known as Wienermobiles, the buses are usually found touring the U.S. to promote the Oscar Mayer food brand. The 2025 race was the first-ever Wienie 500. Each wheeled wienie represented a U.S. region. The South's "Slaw Dog" crossed the finish line first, with all the others left trying to *ketch*-up!

Peanut GALLERY

Artist Brock Davis draws detailed pictures on the inside of peanut butter jars!

Brock, from Minneapolis, starts with a nearly empty jar. He uses a red marker to sketch a guide on the outside. Then he traces the sketch by removing the peanut butter on the inside of the jar. He does this with long tools like butter knives and chopsticks. Using this method, Brock has created detailed copies of famous paintings. The *Mona Lisa* took him about three hours to make. *The Last Supper* took about a week!

The Last Supper

PB MASTERPIECE INSIDE A JAR!

Girl with the Pearl Earring

Mona Lisa

STINKY STAR

A plant in Sydney, Australia, known as Putricia was given the royal treatment when it was about to bloom!

Putricia is a corpse flower. The plant only blooms once every few years, for just one or two days. So, Putricia was placed behind a red velvet rope prior to its rare bloom! A mix of "putrid" and "Patricia," the flower's nickname comes from its awful smell. Some say it smells like rotting meat or stinky socks. But that didn't stop visitors! In January 2025, more than 27,000 people visited the Botanic Gardens of Sydney to see this rare sight. And more than 1.5 million tuned in to watch on a live video stream!

FACT FILES

Corpse flowers are native to Indonesia. Their blooms are some of the largest in the world and can grow up to 9 feet (2.7 m) tall! Their stench attracts beetles and flies, which help spread the flower's pollen.

Growth Spurt

Boys on Indonesia's Nias Island leap into adulthood—literally! Hombo Batu, or stone jumping, is practiced by boys aged 10 and older. The goal is to jump barefoot over stacks of stones up to 6.5 feet (2 m) tall—without touching them! Children practice by jumping over short stacks and adding more stones over time. The tradition started as a way for warriors to prove their courage and strength. Why would warriors need this skill? To jump over enemy walls, of course!

DECEMBER 12 ↗ INTERNATIONAL SOUND

HULA HOOPLA!

Andrea M. is a hula-hooping extraordinaire, using all parts of her body—including her butt!

The London-based performer wasn't always so skilled in the sport. But one day she saw a girl hula-hooping and thought it looked fun. Andrea tried it and has never looked back! Nowadays she goes by Andrea Hulamyhoop, and you can find her performing all sorts of stunts. She even spun a hoop on her butt 453 times before dropping it! Andrea believes she's gotten so good because of her career as a scientist. Her education helps her understand how to balance and move her body with the hoops.

BEARD RULE ↗ For 49 years, New York Yankees baseball players were not allowed to grow beards. The rule was introduced in 1976 by then-owner George Steinbrenner to encourage discipline among the players. It remained in place until his son Hal amended it in 2025.

CRAMMED CONE ↗ Road workers in São Paulo, Brazil, rescued a man who was stuck inside a traffic cone. They were removing cones from the area when they realized that one was much heavier than the others and found a man folded up inside. He said he had squeezed his body into the cone to find shelter from a rainstorm but was then unable to free himself once the storm had passed.

BANANA FEAR ↗ Swedish government minister Paulina Brandberg has a phobia of bananas. Every room she visits has to be banana-proofed beforehand. Her staff makes sure that she never sees or comes into contact with the fruit while performing her official duties.

Bike Flight

Polish inventor Tomasz Patan created a flying motorbike! The Volonaut Airbike weighs just 67 pounds (30.4 kg). It uses jet engines, rather than propellers or rotors, to fly. Although it can't travel very far yet, it can reach an impressive speed of 63 mph (101.4 kmph). You'd be able to out-fly some birds, and you don't even need a pilot's license to do it! However, you will need a cool $880,000 to own this sci-fi sensation.

TWO LINCOLNS Abraham Lincoln had a second cousin who was also named Abraham Lincoln. And they fought on opposite sides during the U.S. Civil War! Private Abraham B. Lincoln served with the Confederates in the 1st Virginia Cavalry.

SINK THEFT A thief stole a sink from the women's restroom of a restaurant in Altrincham, England. She walked into the restaurant and headed straight for the bathroom. She then carefully removed the sink and its pipe. Twelve minutes later, she walked out with the $200 sink hidden in her bag. The restaurant owner said he was used to customers stealing things, but he had never lost a sink before.

NUMBER OBSESSION Serbian-American inventor Nikola Tesla was obsessed with the number three. He would walk three times around the block before entering a building and often washed his hands three times in a row. He also made it a rule only to stay in hotel rooms with a room number that could be divided by three. He died in room 3327 of the New Yorker Hotel.

Earth Heart

There's a lake that's shaped like a heart and filled with blood-red water! Nicknamed the "heart of the Earth," it's found in Inner Mongolia's Tengger Desert. It's also called Wulan or Ulan Lake, after the Mongolian word for "red." It is far off the beaten path, but there are special guided tours for curious travelers. The lake's red color comes from the high amount of salt, metals, and microbes in the water.

Hand-Carved HOME

In the late 1800s, carpenter and artist Karl Junker built his own house and filled it with hundreds of hand-carved objects he made himself!

Known as the Junkerhaus, this one-of-a-kind home is in Lemgo, Germany. It took two years to build, and construction was finished in 1891. But Karl wasn't done. He spent the rest of his life—just over two decades—decorating the inside! He put his carpentry skills to good use and handmade *everything*. He carved detailed wooden panels for every inch of the walls and even the stairs. He made every piece of furniture—chairs, desks, beds, cabinets, you name it. Junkerhaus is now a museum, displaying hundreds of woodwork creations. You have to *cedar* it to believe it!

Ornate wooden sculptures cover every surface, even the stairs!

ALL CARVED BY HAND!

Squeaky Spines

The lowland streaked tenrec has special spines on its back that it uses to make noise! These small mammals are found on the forest floor of Madagascar. Young tenrecs can easily get distracted and wander off. Mom calls them back by rubbing her spikes together—just like a cricket! It gives off a high-pitched sound so her young can find their way back home. This technique is called stridulation, and tenrecs are the only mammals in the world that use it!

EXHIBIT NO. 21691

Katar Dagger

This dagger has a secret blade that appears when you squeeze the handle! It is a type of katar, an ancient weapon dating back to the 1500s in India. They are also known as punch daggers, due to how you grip the handle in a fist. There are many types of katar. This scissor style was likely decorative, but some think it could have been used to inflict greater damage!

TRIPLE THREAT!

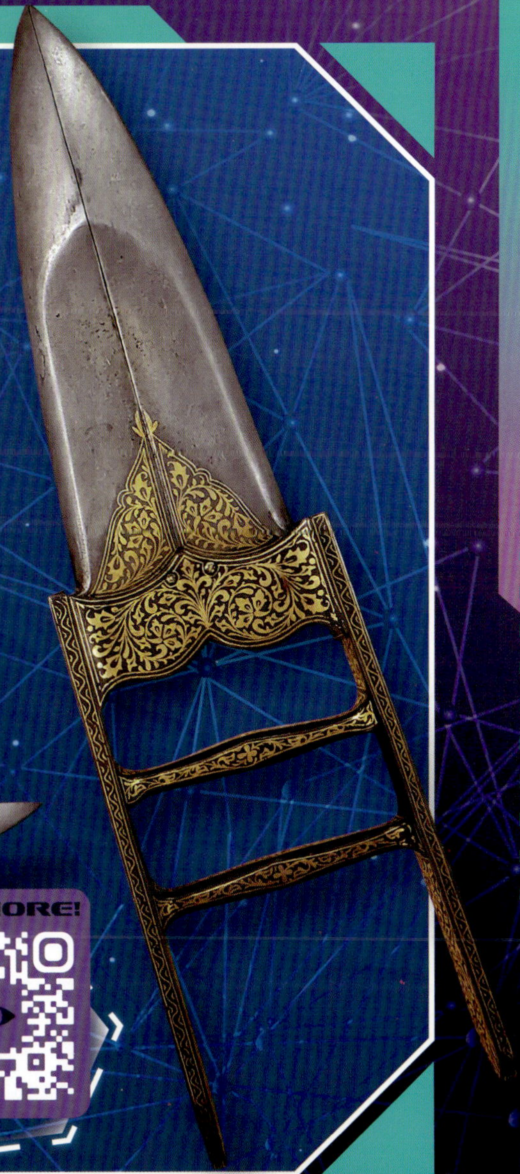

SEE MORE!

SOCCER SIBLINGS Reece James has played soccer for England's senior national men's team, and his sister Lauren has played for the England senior national women's team.

THREE POINTERS Basketball ace Ryan Martin shot 1,134 three-pointers in 56 minutes in Naples, Maine. He averaged one successful basket from behind the three-point line every three seconds.

BASEBALL FIRST Danny Jansen made Major League Baseball history in 2024. He became the first man to play for two different teams in the same game. He was batting for the Toronto Blue Jays on June 26 when heavy rain at Boston's Fenway Park led to the game being suspended in the second inning. By the time the teams met back up to finish the game on August 26, Jansen had signed with the Blue Jays' opponents, the Boston Red Sox. And he reentered the game as the catcher for the Red Sox.

SEVEN WONDERS Egypt's Magdy Eissa visited all Seven Wonders of the World in less than a week. He started at the Great Wall of China before moving on to the Taj Mahal in India, Petra in Jordan, the Colosseum in Italy, the statue of Christ the Redeemer in Brazil, Machu Picchu in Peru, and finally the ancient Mayan city of Chichén Itzá in Mexico. Although the ultimate challenge was carried out in just 6 days, 11 hours, and 52 minutes, it took him nearly a year and a half to plan his itinerary! In between plane rides, he only used public transportation to navigate his journey.

AX THROWER Turkey's Osman Gürcü has a powerful overarm throw. He can hit a target with an ax from a distance of more than 180 feet (55 m). That's further than the length of an Olympic swimming pool!

Rainy Remix

A wall of dull drainpipes in Germany was turned into a musical marvel! Found in the city of Dresden, the bright blue wall is covered in twisty pipes and shiny funnels. When it rains, water runs through the zigzag setup. Before long, the splashing and clanging noises make a melody. Rainy days sure are fun in Dresden!

REVERSE RACE

During the nine-day, 1,423-mile (2,290.2-km) Tour de France car race in 1899, French driver Fernand Charron lost the forward transmission gear on his vehicle. So he turned the car around and drove in reverse for the next 25 miles (40.2 km)!

AFRICAN ADVENTURE Russell Cook ran the entire length of Africa in 352 days, covering more than 10,190 miles (16,399.2 km) and passing through 16 countries. He set off from South Africa's most southerly point in April 2023 and reached the northern tip of Tunisia just under a year later, having run more than a marathon distance each day. He decided to cross the Sahara at night to avoid the harsh daytime heat and sandstorms.

MUSHROOM MUSIC Tarun Nayar can make music from mushrooms. The Canada-based musician connects cables from a home-built synthesizer to plant leaves, trees, and fungi. The machine then turns their natural bioelectric signals into musical notes. He can adjust the knobs and buttons on the synthesizer to create different rhythms.

Head Lights

Artist Kate Schroeder from Missouri lights up her customers' days—with lamp earrings!

The quirky jewelry went viral online, and each release now sells out in minutes. The tiny lamps can be switched on and off. When the batteries run out, they're easy to replace. Kate handcrafts the earrings herself. She can make about 20 earrings in a day. They come in styles like modern, retro, and stained-glass. What a great way to truly "brighten up" your day!

CHILLING CHAPEL

Nestled in the busy city of Milan, Italy, is San Bernardino alle Ossa—a church filled with human bones and skulls!

The church is thought to have the remains of up to 3,000 people in it. The walls are lined with bones and skulls to create awe-inducing patterns. There are multiple cross designs that took hundreds of skulls to create. It was given the nickname "The Bone Chapel." Its history dates to the early 1200s. It was built as an ossuary, which is a building for storing bones when a cemetery becomes full and needs to make room for new burials. Several hundred years later, the remains were used to decorate the church. Travelers come from all over the world to see the unique chapel.

STICKY SCARE ↗ Anna Smith Higgs from England has pittakionophobia, an irrational fear of sticky notes and labels. She often finds herself trembling when she encounters stickers on food items in stores and refuses to eat bananas because they have stickers on their peels.

COLD DRAFT ↗ English scientist Sir Isaac Newton was also a Member of Parliament, where his only recorded comment was to request that a window be closed because there was a cold draft in the chamber.

PHONE FALL ↗ A passenger's cell phone still worked after falling 16,000 feet (4,876.8 m) to the ground from an Alaska Airlines flight. The iPhone landed on a roadside in Portland, Oregon, and was found to be in perfect condition.

BUG BOARDER ↗ A 64-year-old woman in Taiwan experienced constant rustling sounds in her ear, and when doctors investigated, they found a spider living there—next to a discarded exoskeleton it had molted.

GOLDEN TICKET ↗ In 2024, Matthew Ables was able to gain admission to Disney World in Orlando, Florida, with an unused $8 "golden ticket" from 1978.

ATTORNEY ACE ↗ A man in Kenya was accused of impersonating an attorney and representing clients in 26 cases. And even though he wasn't a real lawyer and had never been to law school, he won all 26.

OBVIOUS CHOICE ↗ In 2023, English professional soccer club Walsall, nicknamed "The Saddlers," appointed Mat Sadler as their new manager.

SCHOOL TWINS

In June 2024, 23 sets of twins (plus one girl whose twin brother went to another school) graduated from Pollard Middle School in Needham, Massachusetts. They made up around 10 percent of the eighth-grade class—more than three times the national average.

Cutting Edge

For many years, this chair was thought to be a torture device—but it's not. It was used during special ceremonies by Chinese spirit mediums known as tang-ki. During the ceremonies, it is believed gods take over the mediums' bodies. They do things like pierce their skin, climb ladders made of swords, and sit on bladed chairs. Despite the damage to their bodies, the mediums appear to feel no pain. These acts are meant to show the power of the gods. This practice is still done today in places like Singapore.

SEE MORE!

OUR MOST EXPENSIVE EXHIBIT EVER!

EXHIBIT NO. 176335

Striking Gold

Meet what is probably the shiniest toilet ever made! Artist Maurizio Cattelan created a working toilet called *America* that is 220.5 pounds (100 kg) and made of 18-karat gold. Ripley's bought the golden throne in 2025 for $12.1 million. And if the toilet breaks? Well, it could be melted down and sold for the price of the gold! That was the likely fate of an earlier version of the toilet, which was stolen in 2019.

EXHIBIT NO. 10928

Going Nuts

Charles F. Billat from Ohio carved a tiny toilet out of a walnut shell! It is less than 3 inches (7.6 cm) wide, with an open lid. Charles took up wood whittling after his wife passed. He later moved on to carving nut shells, with walnuts being his favorite!

EXHIBIT NO. 176152 & 176233

Roll with It

An empty toilet paper roll becomes a tiny world in Anastassia Elias's hands. Using just tweezers, glue, and paper, she builds small scenes within the rolls. Her art includes dinosaurs, city streets, and even an amusement park!

INDEX

RIPLEY'S GETS YOU WIRED INTO...
WEIRD
RIPLEY'S Believe It or Not!®
EXPLORE THE EXTRAORDINARY!
WONDER
RIPLEY'S® AQUARIUMS
Find a Ripley's Attraction Near You!

Swing into Fun!
WHIMSY
Ripley's Crazy Golf
Dive into Adventure!
WILD
Have Your Mind Blown!
Ripley's Illusion Lab